Praise for *Grammie Camp*

Grammie Camp is a beautiful book that offers powerful happiness, strategies, and wisdom about infants that will help you nourish a baby's heart. Whether you're a grandmother, godmother, friend, or special auntie, your modelling of happiness is a gift to any baby and the world.

Marci Shimoff,
#1 NY Times bestselling author,
Happy for No Reason, and *Chicken Soup for the Woman's Soul*

GRAMMIE CAMP

A GUIDE FOR ADVENTURES WITH YOUR GRANDBABIES

HEATHER HOBBS

Copyright © 2023 by Heather Hobbs

Grammie Camp
A Guide for Adventures with Your Grandbabies

All rights reserved.
No part of this work may be used or reproduced, transmitted, stored, or used in any form or by any means graphic, electronic, or mechanical, including but not limited to photocopying, recording, scanning, digitizing, taping, Web distribution, information networks or information storage and retrieval systems, or in any manner whatsoever without prior written permission from the publisher.

Edited by Laurie Knight
Cover Design by Kristina Edstrom

An Imprint for GracePoint Publishing (www.GracePointPublishing.com)

GracePoint Matrix, LLC
624 S. Cascade Ave, Suite 201
Colorado Springs, CO 80903
www.GracePointMatrix.com
Email: Admin@GracePointMatrix.com

SAN # 991-6032

Library of Congress Control Number: 2023939040

ISBN: (Paperback) 978-1-955272-85-8
eISBN: 978-1-955272-84-1

Books may be purchased for educational, business, or sales promotional use.
For bulk order requests and price schedule contact:
Orders@GracePointPublishing.com

Dedication

Dedicated to Jacob, the inaugural Grammie camper who inspired the journey, and to his Grandy (Grandpa Randy), who left this world before Jacob arrived but would have been a most excellent grandparent.

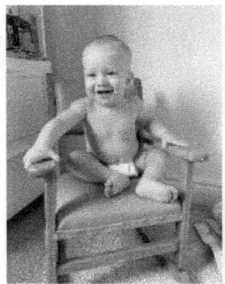 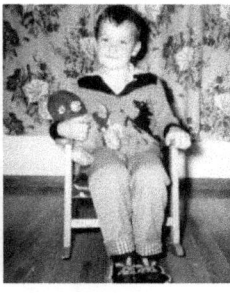  

Sixty years apart, the smiles and the chair are the same.

Grandy loved his Royal Canadian Mounted Police service.

He is a ninth generation Canadian (and future Mountie?)

Also dedicated to all Grammies—by blood, choice, or circumstance—past, present, and future who impart their wisdom and joy to their grandbabies.

Grandmom happily overseeing newer generations.

Great Grandma says to celebrate everyone and every occasion.

Nana rejoices in grandmotherhood.

Babies blessed with four generations of interactions are extra special.

Table of Contents

Foreword ix

Introduction xi

Chapter 1 Grandmother Niche 1

Chapter 2 Grandbaby 11

Chapter 3 Dyad Dynamics 19

Chapter 4 Triad Triumphs 27

Chapter 5 Communication Cues 45

Chapter 6 Grandmothers Share Wisdom 59

Introduction to Chapters 7 to 11 Adventures in Learning Through the Senses 67

Chapter 7 Adventures in Hearing 71

Chapter 8 Adventures in Sight 77

Chapter 9 Adventures in Touch 83

Chapter 10 Adventures in Taste 89

Chapter 11 Adventures in Smell 99

Chapter 12 The End of One and Beginning of Two 105

References 111

Author Accolades 112

Foreword

The joy of being a grandmother dances through the pages of Heather Hobbs' *Grammie Camp*. We who grandmother in myriad ways, from direct line, aunt, or close family friend, etc., are not *JUST* grandmothers but integral to our grandbabies' early development.

Hobbs reminds us again and again that our potential impact for good in our grandbaby's first year of life lasts forever: a sobering and empowering challenge! Thankfully, she includes many practical ways to understand and foster that impact. How empowering and comforting to realize that even if we live far from our grandbabies, today's technology allows us to create these deep bonds in ways unavailable to previous generations.

Beyond sharing her relationship with her own grandbaby, Hobbs brings her wide-ranging experience as a community health nurse working with moms and babies in both Alberta and Ontario to these chapters.

She emphasizes that play is babies' work and not just fun ways to pass the time. Play is essential for baby's psychosocial and language development. In fact, the 1975 Still Face Experiment showed that without at least one consistent nurturing human caregiver, a baby fails to thrive and may not even survive. Communication begins with the first touch and smile and how fortunate is the baby whose grandmother can be part of that consistent foundation. So, while play is fun and often nonsensical, it is extremely important and needs to be intentional. Fitting suggestions for many grammie personality styles and circumstances fill these pages. The examples are inclusive, reaching out to two-person and lone-parent families, traditional and non-traditional couples—there is not one *right* way to be a family or a grandmother!

Heather Hobbs's experience is evident in her chapter on PPMD—post partum mood disorder. She names it as a very real condition that requires help. Unfortunately, many mothers feel shame when they are not sailing through new motherhood, and it is comforting to be told that PPMD is not made up and that it is treatable.

There is so much more wisdom to be discovered in this little book!

As a grandmother of six wonderful young adults, I stand in awe of the grandmothers of sub-Saharan Africa, who, while grieving the loss their own children to AIDS, are bravely raising their orphaned grandchildren. The Stephen Lewis Foundation's Grandmothers-to-Grandmothers Campaign has created a sisterhood of grandmothers across two continents and the awareness that whatever one's circumstances, to be a grandmother is one of life's greatest joys and responsibilities.

Thank you, Heather, for calling us to be miraculous grandmothers!

Catherine Gross,
Aurora, Ontario

Gran Aurora (a chapter of the Grandmothers-to-Grandmothers Campaign established in 2006)

Introduction

Once I joined the grand circle of grandmothers, I developed a heightened awareness of the potential power of my role in influencing not only my grandson's joy, health, and development, but also our mutual happiness and my own renewed curiosity and wonder. Having witnessed other grandmothers in action as well as reflecting on my varied roles of observer, educator, neighbour, friend, community health nurse, camp nurse, theatre volunteer, and theatre-goer—I noticed a huge array of experiences shared with babies. I now wonder if we take grandmothers for granted.

Grandmothers are a valuable resource, and perhaps largely shortchanged in the accolades within themselves and society for the significant impact they can have on their grandbabies. I say grand*babies* because that is the foundation stage and the one addressed in this book. With so many extended family configurations, you may be a grandmother without having been a mother yet still contribute greatly. Clearly, there are also many mothers who are without partners—by choice or not, male or female, or co-mothering (regardless of gender). I am writing to you as one grandmother to another, whether you are biological, legal through adoption, or being treated as a grandmother whether another exists or not.

As a university-educated community health nurse in urban, suburban, and rural communities, and as a childbirth educator, I have served individuals and families for almost four decades as a teacher, resource, advocate, and support in their launching the adventure of parenting. Pregnant or mothering clients ranged from fourteen to seventy-four (a grandmother raising an infant through toddler stage and until six, at which age our program ended). Family visitors served a crucial role in the team effort to foster healthy infants and families during the government funded home visiting program. Visits by both public health nurses (who planned nurse as well as family visitor interventions) and family visitors developed rapport in this therapeutic relationship as caregivers gained confidence in themselves. Often, a grandmother was engaged in the visit and very grateful for the education and support afforded to the family unit. People of many ages, stages, cultures, and languages (fifty-four languages spoken in our region!) welcomed us as allies.

My husband and I raised three stellar individuals, and they all thrive.

My grandson chose his parents well, and he is thriving. He also benefits from not one but two grandmothers as well as a great grandmother. Lucky boy!

How are you doing in your journey?

Grandmothers, my hope is that this book will honour, celebrate, and elevate you. May your talents and contributions in the multiple roles you play under the grandmother umbrella be better recognized and your wisdom shared and appreciated. I hope you glean new ideas herein and are inspired to share your own. Transform your self-image from being "just a grandmother" to a "WOW grandmother," an impactful grandmother tooting your own horn and empowering others to do the same.

I challenge all grandmothers to see themselves as the power source they are—Grammie Power! I propose one way is through something I call Grammie Camp.

No, Grammie Camp is not a place; it's many places. It is a mindset; any place grandmother and grandbaby are together. There is so much more to life than infancy, and if we build the foundation well, life is good.

You have wisdom and knowledge from life experience that will enhance baby's learning. Many inner resources are at your fingertips. May this book validate your perspective. You have power and influence to make a significant impact on your grandbaby's health and happiness and increase your own and the world's happiness—one grandmother and one baby at a time. You can think of yourself as a midwife, birthing a new contribution to the world. Share your brilliance and the joys of your version of Grammie Camp because you have ideas others will not.

The tenets of Grammie Camp include look, listen, pause, go.

So, let's go!

Chapter 1
Grandmother Niche

The noblest art is that of making others happy.

P. T. Barnum

Grandmothers, you are needed!

When my first grandbaby was in utero, I was asked what I would like to be called. Because there was already a Nana, Grandma, Grandmom, Baba, and Granny in the family, I chose Grammie. After dubbing myself Grammie, I created the term *Grammie Camp* as purposeful interactions between myself and my grandbaby, whether at my house, his house, or out and about on adventures. As a camp nurse for young children for almost three decades, I know the value of adventures with much creativity, fun, and imagination. Play is a child's work and conducive to the release of beneficial hormones that signal happiness. Endorphins, which include adrenalin, are often called the happy hormones, but three additional ones are crucial for happiness; they are dopamine, serotonin, and oxytocin. Dopamine is released when goals are achieved. A shopaholic's temporary happiness from a purchase can equate to an infant's success with finally scaling the mountain of a living room chair all by himself! Serotonin is released when we give or do for others with the goal of giving back and connecting with others as opposed to benefit to self. Money can't buy happiness, but that money can be part of philanthropy and elevating someone else's mood or situation. The joy of giving can be on a small, non-monetary scale. Often, we assume extra rich people are extra happy. Alas, making money without making connections may afford temporary happiness but not the kind that fills the heart and just makes a person feel good for helping someone out of brotherly or sisterly love. Longevity and happiness tend to include service to others and faith in a higher being. We humans are meant for connection. We need to think of or pray for individuals, the supports around them, and the supports around the supports. That could be the baby, the nuclear family, the extended family, and the community, be it friends or services.

Oxytocin has been called the love chemical, released with physical contact with a person or pet we cherish. Even in an infant, the tenderness in seeing the family dog can be visible. It is released during breastfeeding and with a kiss or hug with someone we deeply care about. A comforting hand on someone's shoulder can elicit oxytocin release. I felt a rush when my young grandson twiddled the hair at the back of my neck and when he gave his first rudimentary kiss. We may expect nothing in return for our tiring (not tire*less*!) caring for a baby, yet there are many chemical inducing moments to reward us. The ongoing flow of these four chemicals—serotonin, oxytocin, dopamine, and endorphins—is crucial for happiness. As a grandmother, you can turn up the flow.

Imagine there is a miraculous grandmother.
Imagine it is YOU!

Your potential impact for good in your grandbaby's first year of life lasts forever. You can be a catalyst for vast learning that is both subtle and dramatic and beyond your imagination or expectation. If your dream is to become a stellar grandmother, it's yours for the giving, yours for the taking; claim your spot! Time to kick-start your Grammie Power. You and your grand are lucky to have each other, and with appropriate efforts, this baby can grow healthier in heart, body, mind, spirit, and soul. At the same time, you will seem to have more vitality with your renewed sense of value, purpose, and curiosity as you look through the eyes of a baby who shares wonder at this world rich in novel experiences.

There are times in life you may feel it would take a miracle to solve a problem. The most amazing miracle of all is life itself. Imagine this: you feel totally inadequate in your new role as grandmother, you go to sleep, and you wake up knowing something happened. You are unaware of a change (since you were sleeping when it occurred), and yet it transpired. You feel totally prepared and confident interacting with your grandbaby. You awaken and begin to function as that new version of you as a miracle-working grandmother. What's the first thing *you* notice?

What do your grandbaby and his parents perceive as new or somehow different?

How do you act, speak, feel?

What's the first value you would impart to your grandbaby? You may say you don't know. American psychotherapist Insoo Kim Berg found power in some version of the follow-up question she would ask: But if you *did* know (and I know you don't), what would this miraculous grandma of you be like—be doing, saying?

One of the most exciting and gratifying experiences for me is witnessing "aha" moments. A baby can express surprise, joy, and awe with every new experience—be it ever so humble or accidental, like the first time rolling over occurs. This baby could be called an awesome and "aha-some" miracle in motion, and you may be the impetus to get him rolling.

In an atmosphere of isolation and a culture of elders being undervalued as a demographic, grandparents or elders often feel unimportant and superfluous. The result is that the mutually nurturing grandmother/grandbaby relationship can be negated or not encouraged to blossom to full potential.

If ever there was a crucial time for grandmas to up their game, to invest in their grandbaby's happiness and full-spectrum health, it is now.

Grandmothers, you are needed!

As a community health nurse of almost four decades, I have witnessed the sad outcome of caregivers not knowing what to do to engage baby. The Bible says, "My people are destroyed for lack of knowledge" (Hosea 4:6, King James Bible). I have also witnessed and experienced the joy of what planned coaching, intervention, and support can do to power up baby's development. Timely, age-appropriate interactions have an impact. More of these have increased benefit. So, you are very knowledgeable. Hurrah! Alas, knowing is no benefit to baby unless you put it into action.

Happy babies invite happy interactions. Animated grandma faces are the best "toys" around. (Expressive parent and sibling faces are superb as well.) Happy babies are calmer, and they learn better when enjoying themselves. We all do. How wonderful it would be if learning at every age were done in an encouraging, enjoyable environment. Your efforts can boost the happiness baseline for both you and your grandbaby.

Of all the habits to cultivate, happiness is an excellent priority. Happiness is a habit which, unpractised, can be lost. Love is not about getting something but about giving it. Control does not equal love. Some clever anonymous writer asked, "How do you spell love? Answer: T-I-M-E." Giving time, specific and immediate praise (so reason for praise is understood), focused attention, adventures, smiles, hugs, and play—all with safe parameters to explore what piques baby's interest—is a winning combination. It's giving because you want to, rather than just to please someone to earn their love or approval. When you believe and live this, you can help baby believe in himself. Finding his thumb to self-soothe, getting finger food into his mouth, and finding his own toes can all be responded to as remarkable.

Babyhood is fleeting.

It is boggling to witness the speed of change in baby's abilities from week to week and month to month. It's no wonder working parents worry they will miss something. They will. Luckily, there are a zillion firsts to witness. Parents may just be out for a much-valued walk and return to hear from you that baby just took his first steps. That's okay. There will be another first just ahead that they will witness and that you will miss. Celebrate what you observe whether it's the first time or an improved version.

Both Grammie Camp and effective parenting are about meaningful interactions when you are with baby, and that cannot be every minute of baby's life. If it were, that might be aptly named "smotherlove," which I deem an oxymoron since love includes allowing the freedom to explore. To be a part of so much accomplishment within one year is something to be proud of. So many grandmothers, for varying reasons, are deprived of that experience.

Grandparenting—except when also in a full-time caregiver role—is so different from parenting. It's better! When your own child excels or is an embarrassment, parents tend to feel it's a reflection on them. Typically, humans who hear ten compliments and one criticism will ruminate on the one negative comment. It's just how we are wired. Uniquely, though, grandmothers can look through rose-coloured glasses and deem any foible the result of someone else's doing.

There is no manual for how to be a grandmother. By design, it is not you, Grammie, who decides when that career is launched or in what part of the world. No matter, you can jump right in and invent yourself, try it on, tweak your modus operandi, and spread joy. If your goal is to be happy and help baby be happy and hopefully stay that way into adulthood, you are a success. The milk-and-cookies grandmother image may be replaced by hiking or stepping out into the darkness of night with crickets singing, owls hooting, or silence that is mysteriously different from the darkness indoors.

To your grandbaby, you are a miraculous Grammie because you are you and you pay close attention to him. Be the best version of you. That version of *best* will evolve as the facets of your life change and grow. If babies are not in your comfort zone, think *yet*. Through more interaction, comfort grows, as does your ease in your role. Shakespeare, through Hamlet, said, "Assume a virtue, if you have it not" (act 3, scene 4). In other words, act as if you do until it becomes a habit and a part of who you are. Give your energy, enthusiasm, proximity, mobility, time, varied interactions, experiences, and commitment. Who you are as a grandmother is subject to change, much like grandbabies who keep us humble by changing whenever we think we have them figured out. Just be who you were meant to be. You are never too old to ask for help. Caring people appreciate being asked for input. There is no lack of resources though perhaps a lack of resourcefulness. Grandmothers are as unique as babies, and their interactions will vary accordingly. Remember that love isn't love until you give it away. Yes, there is joy in the giving. Like a boomerang, handled correctly, it always comes back to you.

Remember, with one little squiggle and a little space, IMPOSSIBLE becomes I'M POSSIBLE. Believe in yourself. Believe the universe is there for you and on your side. Not everything that happens to you is by your choice or with your permission, but invariably some good, somehow, can be found, though it may take a long time to show itself. It's often been said that stress is not caused by what happens *to you* but in how you choose to respond to that stress. That is one choice we always have.

I was part of a discussion with self-named Happiness Strategist Monique Rhodes when a brilliant British neuroscientist friend of mine, Dr. Lucianne Dobson, spontaneously created a fitting new word—choosipline—mid-discussion. When we discipline ourselves to make choices thoughtfully, we learn that if we don't like our results in life, we need to look at our choices and choose differently to get different results. More than just a word, I think it's like a philosophy or mindset that I highly recommend embracing. A baby can be given choices by putting two or three finger foods on a highchair tray so he may choose to sample all or have a nibble back and forth. A crawling baby can choose which direction to crawl, which toy to investigate, or whether to pull off his sock and carry it in his mouth. Perhaps he learned it watching his dog retrieve his own toys. Since stress is inherent in growth, you can choose to wear a happy demeanour or one of suffering. Which attitude would you rather be around? When you choose to be positive, that is a superpower and one which can transform into Grammie Power.

As you discover and expand your personal grandmother niche, may your specialty be joyful, reciprocal happiness. While you and your awesome grandbaby share playdates, both planned and impromptu, may you spend a zillion glorious Grammie Camp times together.

Read on and blend your stellar imagination and life experience with the information herein to kick-start a Grammie Power movement!

For your consideration in planning Grammie Camp:

- Choose to be a game-changing grandma.

- Choose to be miraculous. Miracles need not be big.

- Create your own rules. Consult others as able or desired.

- Consider yourself self-employed. It is work, and hopefully, work you love. Though not in dollars, grandmotherhood can make you rich in your return on investment through so many valuable non-material ways.

- Seek out others in the grandmother sisterhood or role models from your experience or memory from media or friends.

- Be the part-time or occasional grandmother figure for a young family who has none.

- Figure out and identify your values. Write them in relation to your grandbaby.

- Ask yourself often: What is a loving thing I can do for me right now? When your cup is full, you have more to share. Perhaps you can enjoy a cup of tea during baby's nap. Also ask: What's a loving thing I can do for my grandbaby when he wakes up? A smile and hug and picking baby up are loving actions.

- Ask yourself on a scale of one to ten what number represents your present level of happiness. That may be your happiness setpoint or baseline. Plan one baby step you can do on your next visit with grandbaby that may raise that number a half or whole point. Soon you will scale mountains and think nothing of it.

- Think of one aha moment you experienced or witnessed with your grandbaby. What made it aha or "aha-some"? Smile and savour that moment for fifteen seconds. A quick internet search yields that research shows smiling increases happiness. Keep your radar on and anticipate many more happy moments to come.

- Keep a gratitude journal. Photos can augment it.

- Practice good body mechanics and posture in any position that baby care requires. Your "mother muscles" may be long gone. Set good habits at the start so Grammie Camp isn't followed by your muscles in misery.

- Practice your story reading voices and facial expressions in front of a mirror or read aloud to a friend. This could become a joyful new habit, even with others beyond your grandbaby.

- Craft your own word or phrase for what you do for Grammie Camp. Rather than phrases like babysitting or minding baby, what words might describe the dynamic person you are and what creativity you bring to the dynamic duo of you and your stellar grandbaby?

Ask yourself, "If I were using my Grammie Power, what would I be doing? If I were a miracle-working grandmother, what might that look like?" Perhaps those are not the right questions and declarations work better for you. Try: "I have Grammie Power. I am a miraculous grandmother, a change maker, and these are but a few of my superpowers! How can I exercise my Grammie Power today?"

A Letter from Grandbaby

Dear Grandma,

I have heard you say that I am very clever for choosing good parents. I agree. I also think I am super clever for choosing you to be my grandma. You are my favourite person in the whole world! You make everything so much fun, and I feel so happy when we are together. I also love that action song we do: "If You're Happy and You Know It, Clap Your Hands!" I can't do the actions myself yet, but I love watching your face as you sing and move my hands and feet at the right times. You sure know a lot of songs and like to show me how to be silly.

Love,

Your Favourite Grandson,

Randy

Even these are big shoes to fill. Every little person has greatness within.

A Loving Limerick

There once was a grandma dubbed Nan
Whose grandbaby's name was young Dan.
They both had such fun,
With both Number ONE,
And each being the other's best fan!

(This limerick is an example of entertaining myself while driving with Grammie Camp in mind. Babies love rhythm and they like being around happiness.)

My family atop Taipei 101, the tallest tower in Taiwan. Tough to top this adventure.

Great Grandma at eighty years young!

Chapter 2
Grandbaby

Be great in little things.

St. Francis Xavier

Is there anyone grander or more soul-nourishing than a happy grandbaby responding to you enthusiastically? A baby who lights up and is delighted to see you? It's miraculous, with all the cell division involved in creation and culminating in birth, that we look anything like one another, but we usually do.

Human infancy is from birth to twelve months. In that time, the brain is taking in messages from all senses: hearing, sight, touch, taste, and smell. It is growing at a rate faster than in future years. With baby's first breath, the brain orchestrates the immediate shift from in-utero absorption of oxygen and nutrients via mom's bloodstream and placenta to the totally new mechanism of breathing air through lungs. The shock of bright light, loud noises, cooler air, non-continuous nutrients, and handling by different people must be a series of trials. Learning to coordinate the suck/swallow/breathe combination is natural, yet not always straightforward. Regulating sleep cycles, digestion, circulation, waste management, body temperature, skeletal development, and much more fortunately has a blueprint. For baby, testing what her body is capable of and realizing, in fact, that it is her body, then being gradually able to direct its movements, are all sources of wonder and effort. The brain triples in size in the first year. This is a crucial time to provide experiences to enhance growth.

Perhaps a baby's thoughts include: *Where am I? What am I? What's happening now? I'm hungry. I'm tired. I'm wet. I'm bored. I'm overstimulated. Oh, thank you, thank you to the big people who are taking care of me!* While grandbaby adapts to our world, we grandmothers adapt to a baby's newness of everything.

During that first year, opportunities abound to set the tone for love.

In 1 Corinthians 13:13, Paul says: "And now abide faith, hope and love, these three; but the greatest of these is love" (New King James Version). Virtually every grandmother I surveyed stated the most important gift to her grandbaby is love. We need air, water, and food, but without at least one consistent nurturing human caregiver, a baby fails to thrive and may not even survive. She needs a caring person in order to later develop the ability to emotionally care for others.

A classic research experiment by Harry Harlow involving infant rhesus monkeys kept one baby with its mother and one isolated and deprived of its mother, who was replaced with a frame of wire and wood with a bottle, so milk was easily accessible. That second chimp had the basics of air, water, and food, but in lacking a breathing, heart-beating caretaker, it died. It was a groundbreaking psychology experiment that demonstrated the value of maternal connection, which, of course, begged the question of humans responding in a like manner.

We now know babies can be depressed, fail to thrive, or even die, but most learn the world is not a welcoming, safe place if they don't feel care and love.

A young man, unmarried and not a father, visited a mutual friend when I had a clever one-year-old. Since the man was annoyingly expounding on his theories of parenting, I asked at what age he thought one can get a response or feedback from a baby or child. He was taken aback and finally answered, "Nine?" I can only hope that if he later became a father, he learned that's not true. A newborn baby gives us feedback. Mostly that looks like crying or sleeping or eating. We just haven't learned her language yet.

Message sent doesn't necessarily mean message received. When her needs are met, she lets you know. When her needs are not met, she lets you know. If lying on a bed with an adult, a newborn can wriggle over to the warm body. A famous photograph of premature twins in an incubator captured the stronger twin putting an arm over the weaker twin's back. Just because we don't understand something doesn't mean it's not happening.

Grammie Camp is purposeful interactions that foster and enhance baby's growth and development. That includes physical, emotional, cognitive, social, and spiritual growth. How you interact overall with your grandbaby will set the tone for relationships, curiosity, sense of self, as well as her opinion about the world she is part of. We all have days we don't bring our best selves to the situation; hence it is the overall presence and impact that matters.

An English proverb states, "Necessity is the mother of invention." Given the improvisation required by mothers, my own mom used to quip the reverse, saying, "Mother is the necessity of invention." Be it shortage of money or time or strength, your ingenuity is often called upon. On your best days, as well as on mediocre energy ones, you may choose or invent ways to energize Grammie Camp while conserving your own physical or emotional energy.

A grandbaby is a grand responsibility, a blessing, an opportunity, and it carries potential for significant rewards for her, her family, and eventually, society. She is worth the investment. Your Grammie Camp endeavours can have a far-reaching impact on her personality, her joy, and her happiness, and yours as well. You can provide experiences that are developmentally appropriate for each age. Being there, watching and tuning in to her actions will help you learn and know what is good for her. Just as a one-month-old cannot possibly walk, a ten-month-old baby isn't interested in staying in one place for long.

"To fail to plan is to plan to fail," said Benjamin Franklin and many others since. So, be a planner for Grammie Camp. Act on your plan. Expect success. Think trial and success. A wise grandmother said, "Failure is not the opposite of success. It is part of success." A Japanese proverb says, "Fall seven times, stand up eight." You weren't born knowing how to be a grandmother, but your grandbaby doesn't know that. Just do your best, considering all your influencers of today. Tomorrow will be another brand-new day to be enough exactly as you are. No need to be perfect. An impactful daily mantra from Monique Rhodes who I agree is The Happiness Strategist is: "I love myself. I take care of myself. I am enough just as I am." This is a good guide to emulate and impart.

Reclaim your childlike curiosity. One of the perks of being with a baby is that we look at the world differently, with more of a sense of awe. In 1 Corinthians 13:12, Paul says, "When I was a child, I spoke as a child, I understood as a child, I thought as a child; but when I became a man, I put away childish things." How wonderful that Grammie Camp invites a return to appreciating childish things. Paul's wisdom also reminds me that a child is not a mini-adult. Happy child experiences and relationships do foster happiness in adults.

A baby is not just a blob. She is dependent, yet her senses are alert and taking in all the world has to offer or missing out on all it does not offer. There's an infamous song, "Cat's in the Cradle" by Harry Chapin, in which a boy keeps asking his dad to come play and dad keeps saying soon, soon. Eventually, the boy grows into a man. The dad now has time and asks his son to get together and, as you may guess, the son unconsciously though politely does what his dad modelled and says something like, "Not now, but we'll get together real soon." Then, sadly, the father realizes his son turned out just like him. Repetition seals in learning. An infant has not yet developed consciousness, but her subconscious (like yours) is taking in all stimuli and assigns them meaning as good, bad, or neutral. What messages will baby absorb while in your care?

Babies read what we DO. If we say "I love you" but are frowning and have an edge to our voice, the body language means more to baby than the words. Likewise with adults.

There are many learning styles, as well as personality and character traits. Dominantly auditory learners need to hear new information, visual learners need to see it, kinesthetic learners need to do it. You and your grandbaby may have differing learning styles, so do your best to incorporate all three. There's a Confucian saying, later repeated by Benjamin Franklin, that will be a helpful Grammie Camp guideline: "Tell me, and I forget. Teach me, and I may remember. Involve me, and I learn."

You and your grandbaby will flourish in calm, safe settings as you explore and discover abilities, your duo dynamics, and the joys and challenges of interactions. It's up to you to set the stage and seize opportunities when they arise.

You may have a grand plan for your two hours of Grammie Camp only to find she sleeps the entire time. Rather than feel disappointed, consider for what reason you may have been redirected. Perhaps Mom needs your company today more than baby does. If Mom is happy, that helps the whole family be happy.

There is a plethora of resources available for infant development and activity ideas (some are listed later in the book). Be a seeker of ideas and knowledge. Then be a doer and sharer. Your special grandbaby is a sponge for your love and attention.

Be there for her. Be actively engaged, even if that means sitting and holding her as she sleeps. That's a worthy reward.

Above all, let her know often she is special and loved in many ways. For a baby, that is the ultimate gift.

Some Grammie Camp ideas include:

- Respond to baby quickly. Pay attention and you will learn if she wants to be picked up or just woke herself up briefly but was back to sleep before you got to her crib. Responding can mean listening more closely before deciding on the next step.

- Smile often and verbally greet baby.

- Use praising words to describe your grandbaby, like calling her clever or cute, saying, "I love your soft skin and your perfect ten toes," and noticing out loud how baby is problem solving and being curious.

- Reflect verbally what you think baby may be thinking or saying. "Yes, Grammie loves you and is happy to change your diaper so you will feel dry and comfortable."

- When reading a book to baby, relate your baby's name to a lovable character in the book.

- Use baby's stuffed animals to playfully kiss baby's neck or tummy and say baby's name along with kissing sounds.

- Refrain from assigning adult traits to baby. She is not crying with the purpose of bothering you. A baby cries to express a need of someone or something. She is not manipulating you. Her brain is not that developed. Babies whose needs are met don't need to send false signals. Neither do grandmothers!

A Letter from Grandbaby

Dear Nanai Nanai,

You make me feel happy. I don't know how you do it. Even when I have no idea what I want, you seem to know. Someday, I will learn to talk like you do, and I will tell you that thing that makes me feel all snuggly. "Wo aini, I love you."

Love,

Lily

She speaks the universal language.

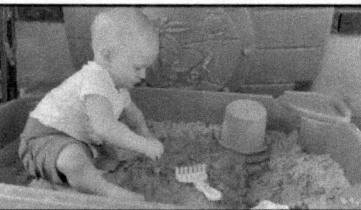

Baby working on his natural immunity.

Baby, pondering his next moves.

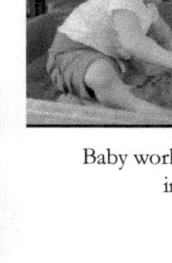

Aren't grandmothers fascinating? They care about us little guys so much.

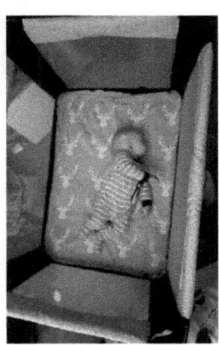

We never wake a sleeping baby!

Chapter 3
Dyad Dynamics

The moment is everything. Don't think about tomorrow; don't think about yesterday: think about exactly what you're doing right now and live it and dance it and breathe it and be it.

Wendy Whelan, American ballet dancer

Dyad = two individuals maintaining a significant relationship.

Dynamics = pattern or process of change, growth, or activity.

    The dyad of grandmother and grandbaby is like two dancers—two playmates moving and responding to each other in ever-evolving ways where some familiar steps intermingle with some new steps at unrehearsed intervals. As this improvisation continues, you will notice in baby's first year the rapid pace of learning in him but perhaps not the nuances of your own shifting in how you are being. While you are *doing*, your greater gift is in *being*.

    Rather than the *I can't* approach, infants appear to embrace the *how can I?* perspective. It's as if they innately believe it's not the never falling or failing (whatever that is!) that culminates in success but the rising, refreshing, and repeating that leads to mastery. Wouldn't it be empowering if we all held that belief? There is a natural drive to learn and grow. You can instill and nurture that in yourself. The more you grow, the more there is to share. Using your unique gifts tends to energize.

According to the Barnard Center for Infant Health and Development, a baby recognizes his mother and father (or others who interact frequently) soon after birth. That trusted caregiver's interactions with comforting efforts support the hypothalamic-pituitary-adrenal (HPA) axis, an important part of the stress response system. External comforting can help baby learn to self-comfort later. When a baby relaxes into your arms, he is saying, *I feel safe with you.*

When you love yourself, you are capable of loving others. If you are not thriving, it is challenging to help someone else do so. Baby's dependence and the steep parental learning curve, combined with sleep deprivation like no other and with a seemingly warped sense of time, together can be best described as intense. Baby is the number-one priority, and all else ranks lower or may fall off altogether as priorities shift. You as grandmother can help alleviate any or all these factors.

When you stop and focus on a new life that is fresh and open with possibilities, you can be a change maker. You are the only one you can change. While rocking a baby or observing his dependence, you have time to reflect on your own life with all its ups, downs, and sidesteps. You can use this time to strategize how to provide baby with crucial learning opportunities, as well as to gift yourself with commitment to continue or begin to fall in love with yourself.

Can you love someone else's baby?

Can you love yourself?

Do you feel you are sacrificing your free time to babysit?

Are you planning your time with baby as you would a much-anticipated vacation?

When you realize the power of time spent sharing the gift of you with your grandbaby, you can be so proud and privileged to have that opportunity.

Whenever baby's health or circumstances present as less than preferred, consider the ever-present option to reframe. Whether something is good or bad is a matter of your mental choice to name it so. What you deem drudgery may be someone else's idea of luxury or fun. If the image you have of grandmothers does not appeal to you, create one you do like and can aspire to. Choose to generate fun in all your teaching.

Discipline is one thing. *Choosipline*, as mentioned earlier, is a necessity that is often not realized; so, the number-one activity to choose for Grammie Camp is play. The essence of play is delight. It is crucial to baby. Play is baby's work. The sounds of play, with giggles and squeals and possibly grunts of exertion or frustration during attempts at new skills, are what draw adults in. Alas, many adults lose this childhood delight, possibly from ill-advised peers shaming them for being childish. Being childlike has some merit, especially if it evokes *joie de vivre*. Therefore, choose play, every day (even without baby). Pediatrician Dr. T. Berry Brazelton guided parents to notice what's right with baby versus problems, and if they want to know what kind of person their baby is, just play with him.

In Eastern culture, *guru* refers to a beloved teacher, a sacred relationship between a teacher and a student. This relationship effects change, which ultimately gives a sense of acceptance and love. So, a committed grandmother is like a guru in teaching spiritual and good-human-being tenets to her grandbaby. Teaching through demonstrating love as unconditional frees baby to be a risk-taker with the security of grandmother at hand.

As a grandmother, you serve many of the same roles as your grandbaby's parent or parents. In general, you may be exempt from night duty and the ultimate disciplinarian role, which may give you an edge in popularity in later years but not so much in infancy. You do have to set some boundaries on what works for you. If baby is teething and chomps on you, clearly give the message that's not okay. If he pulls the dog's hair, redirect his attention to patting and explain what to do. Take baby's hand or stroke the dog and say, "Nice, gentle. Puppy likes it that way."

You are like the tip of the iceberg: hardly visible, one whose magnitude is not seen but is present, nonetheless. Actor Jim Carrey said, "The effect you have on others is the most valuable currency there is." When your presence elicits a smile, a laugh, or a comfort, you are rich enough to share freely.

Grandmotherhood is such an undervalued, untapped resource. Lack of regard for elders is not universal, but often ageism undermines wisdom and elders feel a lack of purpose. Grandmothers come in all ages and stages of life, so generalities risk loss of meaning. Different cultures have different expectations, both of elders and by elders, but…

What if you recognize your potential greatness?

What if you know ways to positively impact a baby's development in body, mind, heart, and spirit?

What would it take to believe fully that you are one of the keys to your grandbaby's awesome destiny?

When you realize that everything is created twice—first as a thought, then as an action or words or a thing—you will realize the power of influence you can have. When you think your grandbaby will smile, you expect him to smile, and he does. You do not force him to smile. You can easily set the stage for the opposite.

You need to hear from yourself what your dream is for your relationship with your grandbaby. The point of the "purposeful" interactions of Grammie Camp is to make sure time is well spent. If you seek to make a difference in his life, *be* a difference. If what you are doing is working well and serving a connection to whatever your purpose is, keep doing it. If interactions are not satisfying, rather than blaming some external person or factor, learn what you can glean from that, then create your new way. You will discover it when you pay attention. As a committed grandmother, in embracing Grammie Camp as spending time *purposefully*, you almost certainly will enhance the degree of happiness for both of you. When you hold your grandbaby and dance or sway or bounce, it's a dance of two different generations. What your grandbaby learns through affectionate, joyful, attentive interactions is who he is—that he is accepted, loved, cared for, and is good enough exactly as he is in this moment. Those are gifts many adults crave. What a blessing to impart them to an infant. Who each of you is next week, next month, or whenever your next visit is, who you both are, will be different than today because you each will have changed. Nothing is static.

There is an Indian proverb that says: "To watch us dance is to hear our hearts speak." If you have music as you dance, hearing that song in the future may bring back the wonderful memory of your young and perfect dance partner. Virtual videos can serve to shrink the distance between you and help relieve Grammie withdrawal. After a few months, he will know your face and voice as if you are there.

You will likely see more dramatic changes in an infant than in yourself. However, as you give, you also gain in subtle ways. Your riches are in values, an income more important than money. Your legacy will live in the person, even if not in the bank. You need not have a high-powered business role to have wealth.

- Refrain from saying, "I'm just a grandmother." No one is a "just a" anything.

- Say, "I am a grandmother!" Next to being a mother, that's your most significant contribution to society.

- When you experience awe in your grandbaby's ability, don't keep it to yourself. Tell baby. "You're so clever! You found your thumb."

- Dance like someone's watching because someone is. Perhaps you are inspiring another grandmother in the making.

- Believe in your greatness. Be humble. Be grateful.

- Believe in your added value to grandbaby. Be his beloved teacher.

- Enjoy. Laugh. Smile. This triggers production of endorphins, the happy hormones. Speak only what you want to happen. No criticism.

- Love grows through loving interactions. Yet it requires intentional action.

- You can do this! Think, see, hear, and feel it. You are doing this.

A Letter from Grandbaby

Dear Grammie,

I am so happy you were chosen to be my very own grandmother. When you see me, your loving smile and sparkling eyes tell me I am a lucky boy. I am excited for our next adventure. Of course, at five months old, everything is an adventure! Mom and Dad have taken me and my "bro" Mac the lab for several snow walks in the woods with the cool sled and buffalo plaid blanket you gave me for Christmas. It's so cozy, and Dad says the sled is a dream to pull. That means more walks! Mom said she sent you pictures. I love going outside, even when it's cold, because I am well bundled up by Mom. Thanks for the sled!

Love,

Jacob, Your Number-One Grandson

Baby and Grammie in winter wonderland. Outdoors in any weather!

Granny and baby basking in "You are my sunshine."

Little one and Nana having fun with Grammie Camp

People watching at a post COVID concert for children.

Nana and baby spending time at eye level.

Cuddles between generations.

Love compounds through the generations when nurtured.

Oma and baby building relationships with play.

Honorary Grandma having fun with her gnome.

Multigenerational joy magnifies love.

Sink baths appeal to all the senses.

Chapter 4
Triad Triumphs

Praise, like sunshine, helps all things to grow.

Croft M. Pentz

Grammie Power is generally trumped by Mommy Power, but rather than trumping, an amicable alliance is in everyone's interests.

The triad I refer to is the grandmother, the baby, and the baby's mother. As you embrace your grandmother role, your mother and mother-in-law roles need to be respectful, encouraging, and empathetic. Adults are no different from babies in the need for praise, confidence-building, and frequent acts of kindness. You may be humble in your offerings or may present as all-knowing and "better than" the mother.

Refrain from giving advice. It may be an unwitting vice!

Have you ever heard a father-in-law joke? Is there such a thing? Perhaps this is because the women are busy being caregivers—mothering the mothers, grandmothering the babies, and trying to do self-care and not step on anyone's toes in the manoeuvring. Stereotypes abound and all have an element of both truth and fabrication. You may have already been established as the ally or the adversary. If the latter is true, resolve to turn that around and act.

Instead of lavishing well-meant advice, ask "How can I be helpful?" Offer suggestions but allow the mother control. It's her baby. A new mom may forget exactly what you say, but she will undoubtedly remember how you make her feel. Every little thing you say, do, or imply about her mothering ability has initial and lasting impact, and your heroine or villain identity begins. Past relationship woes need correction and healing. If not possible to agree to disagree on certain topics, it may be best to find common ground on other matters. This time is an opportunity to strengthen your relationship for the long-term alongside the shared goal of treasuring the masterpiece of *her* baby.

There are so many configurations of this triad. Gone is the so-called norm or stereotype of a baby with a mother, a father, and two grandmothers. There may be three or four grandmothers all jockeying for position in the race to be the most popular. Perhaps you are quite happy to not play a leading-lady role. In any case, where there are people, there are people dynamics, and when change is everywhere, someone who dislikes change may lose the usual niceties.

You have likely learned already that we cannot change others. Not anyone. It doesn't stop us from trying, though. Perhaps tactics change, yet when deep down we don't accept them for themselves, we need to redirect our change-agent desires to none other than ourselves. Consider that whatever they say or do that irks you may be something you also say or do yet have not recognized or acknowledged in yourself. When we change ourselves, for some inexplicable reason, the dynamic changes and the relationship improves. Appreciation, gratitude, and forgiveness from one another all boost happiness, but in this scenario, focus on the giving. They are also important to practice within oneself. It is common to be able to forgive anyone except oneself. Why is that? Unforgiveness can lead to minor and major ailments. Forgiveness does not condone hurtful actions or words. What it does do is prevent damage to the person holding a grudge or wound by allowing it to fester and grow, often having forgotten the original offence.

Consider your grandbaby's mother becoming a mother—no matter how much and how long hoped for, planned for, and experienced through birth or adoption process—there has been a shift in identity. No one can prepare a new mother for the intensity of parenting. You, by just being near and available, can demonstrate your support. If someone is drowning, you can throw out a lifeline, but it is up to them to take it. A multiple-time mother has the advantage of experience, but not with *this* baby and not with the need to divide attention between children. It's a reconfigured learning curve. Likewise, with you, whether helping with one baby or a baby and an older child or just the older child so mom can dedicate attention to baby may be how you can best support the family. You may reflect on your own mothering experience with regrets or triggers; yet you can always choose to focus on the positive memories or how you changed for the better with subsequent intention. Sometimes our worst life experiences prove much later to be gifts to force change and desirable growth. (Though certainly not seen as so at the onset.)

No amount of advance reading or babysitting other people's babies can predict the hormonal upheaval, the emotional pulls, and the natural fears combined with extreme sleep deprivation in the early weeks, months, and often beyond. Fortunate is the mom who functions adequately on five hours' sleep. Research continues to say we need seven hours' sleep to allow the night-time healing and natural waste removal from the body. Fallout from interrupting our circadian rhythm is real. Night shift workers understand this, and mothers are working split shifts all the time. The most often used word I have heard from new parents to describe their new life is "intense." Having been told of this intensity in advance is irrelevant. It must be experienced.

Can you think of any past job you had that called for no prerequisites, offered no training or mentoring, and totally lacked predictability? Welcome to motherhood and the stress of unknown territory, compounded by the challenge of the worst sleep ever. Somehow, though, humanity lives on. I received a cartoon of one stressed hen atop a mountain of eggs with a couple broken eggs at the base. The caption read, "Motherhood is not for wimps." I concur.

Who the new mother was before your grandbaby arrived is forever gone. Even if she's excited and welcoming of the new role, she may feel a subtle undertone of an unidentified unpleasant feeling which could be her grieving the loss of her former self. Simply sharing this observation may ease her fear of non-normalcy. In my community health nurse role, I shared this perspective with a distraught mother who was isolating herself in her bedroom, feeling depressed and misunderstood. Her concerned husband and his mother were banished and confused in the living room. Immediately after our discussion, she called them to her bedroom urgently, accusingly declaring: "See! She understands!" She was so relieved to learn that others had felt that way too.

Depression, grief, and sleep deprivation have a lot in common, with loss being the central issue. If the mother experienced a traumatic birth or there is an unexpected or unwelcome variation in baby's health or mother's well-being, emotional upheaval and potential grieving are not only to be expected but are necessary. You, as grandmother, may feel just as emotionally raw and not know what to say. If that is the case, then saying nothing may be the best. Just be. Just listen. Let there be spaces in your togetherness, but not abandonment. A mother's hormones shift massively within twenty-four hours of birth, so it's no wonder feeling overwhelmed is a common theme.

In my experience, some of the moms smiling most often are the ones hiding depression. They say their friends and acquaintances would be shocked to know of their struggles with anxiety and depression. Assume nothing. Ask Mom how she is feeling today. Somehow specifying "today" elicits a more thoughtful response. Be curious, but not interrogative.

Watch for what Mom is doing well and note it aloud. Saying it to someone in her presence or if she can overhear can lend importance and credence to the compliment. Build trust in small, everyday moments. Be empathetic about her emotions. Stop and ask what she is thinking or feeling today. She may not know. If she expresses anger, don't take it personally. If you triggered her negative response, apologize. Swallow your pride. Forgive her imperfections and forgive yourself yours. Miscommunication is perhaps more common than communication. As stated earlier, message sent does not necessarily mean message received. A broken telephone effect may have occurred somewhere between your mouth and non-verbal cues and her ears or perception. If a comment from her seems hurtful, before reacting, confirm what you think she said. You may have missed a crucial word. Avoid "never" and "always" as in, "You never listen to me" or "You always have to have the last word." True or false, these tend to be inflammatory words.

Postpartum mood disorder (PPMD) is not predictable. Why am I addressing it when our focus is on Grammie Camp? In any family, one member in crisis overflows to the others. Grammie Camp may be hijacked by more pressing needs of baby's ill mom. Common recommendations from mothers after birth was that PPMD should be talked about before birth. Forewarned is forearmed.

In my role as community health nurse, I addressed PPMD in childbirth education classes as well as in postnatal classes and transition-to-parenting groups, but mostly during the home visiting program in Ontario and Alberta, Canada. One mom I met in prenatal classes was attentive but said little. I was also the nurse who visited for breastfeeding support in the first day home postpartum, at her request. She readily confided her desire to have nothing to do with her new baby, though she was committed to breastfeeding. Emotionally, she was a wreck. She had decided in the last trimester to discontinue an antidepressant medication without medical guidance because she learned that her longtime (since her teens) prescribed medication has potential risks to baby in utero or through breast milk. With such a dramatic removal of her mood-stabilizing medication, her body chemistry shift caused her to crash. She could barely cope with herself and said she had nothing to give emotionally to the baby.

Amazingly, she did breastfeed successfully, but did not enjoy it. She had no joy, no intention to care for the baby, with some shame mixed in. Generally, mothers welcome support but don't abdicate their role as primary caregiver, but this mom did. Dad and out-of-province Grandma did everything but nurse the baby until she stabilized and grew to engage with her infant. This first grandbaby experience hugely altered this grandma's imagined joyful supporting role to one of taking on all mothering duties with suicide watch added. The baby's father also wondered what happened to the woman he knew and whether she would return emotionally.

Together, Grandma and baby's dad attended to baby as Mom resumed her medication, this time with medical supervision. The health care team included a community health nurse, family visitor, family doctor, and a psychologist or psychiatrist (to support Grandma as much as Mom). We humans are complex. Mom gradually regained emotional and chemical equilibrium, and two years later chose to have another baby and successfully maintained postpartum wellness.

Even in the absence of depression or anxiety, I have seen instances of a super-helpful grandma visiting and doing everything for a week so Mom can rest. Then the grandma goes home; Mom may now have a week-old baby she knows not how to care for but feels foolish asking for support.

In university, I was taught that in the 1950s, the diagnosis of "postpartum depression" was removed from the diagnoses' manual, claiming there could not be a gender-specific depression. In the early 1980s, I was part of a community health nurse team learning more and teaching about the return to recognition and diagnosis of postpartum depression. Now, it's more commonly broadened to "postpartum mood disorder" (PPMD) since anxiety and depression with occasional psychosis come under the same umbrella. Also, it is recognized that fathers can suffer PPMD, as can adoptive parents. The present DSM-5 (*Diagnostic and Statistical Manual of Mental Disorders*, May 2013) notes the most common mental health disorders in North America are anxiety disorders, major depression, and bipolar disorder. The good news is most mothers do not develop PPMD. Though not predictable and not necessarily repeated with future births, prevention through education, discussion of risks, signs, and symptoms, and anticipatory supports—such as protecting sleep—can help.

As a grandmother, you may notice a mother's change in mood. Encourage her to express her feelings. Create the space for her to process emotions without judgment. Help her realize the impermanence of these emotions. PPMD is temporary when timely and appropriate supports are in place. You can support her sleep, nutrition, and confidence, and help her identify when or if she may need medical involvement. In the rare event of psychosis, you or another adult needs to take charge as delusional thinking and irrational judgment may be part of it. Her doctor or a crisis line can assess. It is not your sole responsibility. Identify and link her with relevant resources. Remember to give baby extra care; babies can feel the emotional climate. It is in the whole family's interest to be attuned to afford early intervention, if needed. Joy does return but hope of that is not seen when one is in the midst of feeling hopeless. You can carry the hope and speak of it until she feels it.

When a friend stated, "I have lost my joy," I was so impacted by her sudden emotional doldrums that I offered these words: "Your joy knows who you are and where you live. Keep the welcome mat out for a return visit." Fortunately, the message resonated with her and elicited her first smile in weeks. Soon after, her unexpected connecting with someone and reliving past joyful memories brought a renewed presence of joy and gratitude. Mindset, more than clock or calendar, is a golden key to our wellness.

In pregnancy, fear of being the one who suffers postpartum mood disorder can add stress to Mom as well. Somewhat encouraging is that just because Mom has a history of depression and recovered does not mean she will have PPMD. The same applies if the grandmother had PPMD. It is not genetic. Not only will Mom have developed coping strategies that allow recovery, but she and others in her inner circle may also have a heightened attention to her mood. Return to wellness occurs more quickly with action, not by ignoring the problem.

As a community health nurse who has often seen recovery and a return to balanced mood, I could share success stories and my belief in her becoming one of them. My work over many years involved hundreds of women who experienced postpartum mood disorder, went through it, and recovered with new self-care strategies to apply long-term. These transferable skills added to their repertoire to cope under stress. That may well be the silver lining and light after the dark days.

As a nurse, I have always believed in promoting healthy habits, and that preventing health problems is in the interests of the individual, the family, and the community. The cost of ill health—physical, mental, emotional, spiritual, and cognitive—is ever rising. We can all do our bit to reverse that.

The short and long-term good that you can do to foster your grandbaby's self-esteem cannot be underestimated. Many health professions link mental health disorders with a lifelong sense of not feeling loved, accepted, or worthy. One of my goals for this book is to increase your happiness and feeling of worthiness!

Resilience is a learnable skill. Baby care is learnable. Noting mother's strides aloud, little by little as her body chemistry stabilizes after birth, is crucial. There is infinite power in praise. She needs to repeatedly hear and feel that she is doing a good job. Most mothers think everyone is coping better than they are.

More good news is that new mothers learn to function on mostly inadequate sleep, aided by their joy as they marvel at their beautiful babies. Once you have a baby, you will be tired for the next how long? Pregnant moms' hopeful answers include weeks or months, but some have been forewarned that it's years. Who needs sleep when you can live on love? Oh, and are there other children or stepchildren? Even the twenty-one-year-old who is accustomed to being the baby in the blended family can resent and exhibit signs of jealousy of the new arrival. More than one firstborn has suggested the baby be sent back. Although the older sibling may have been told there would be a new brother or sister to play with, she may be confused and disappointed once routines have been totally disrupted. Mom's attention has been robbed by the baby who was the intended *fun* playmate. No one likes to be bumped out. Canine and feline family members also need to be included in the introductions and adjustment to the baby. Grandmothers can help in this transition, too, by giving the older sibling or pet some extra attention and fielding insensitive guests who gush over baby and ignore the older child or dog. Helpful, also, is taking the dog for a walk and being sure the cat maintains some sense of routine to avoid stress and acting out on all fronts.

One of my clients brought her Doberman into her marriage. Her husband was not a fan of the dog. When the dog-lover mom was occupied with baby, the dog was not cared for by the also-busy dad. Canine retaliation came in the form of projectile diarrhea all over the house for a couple of days. The dog did not endear himself with Dad. Finally, the devoted mom reached her limit and shouted at the dog, "If you do that one more time, you will be gone!" Guess what? It never happened again. Who knows what went on in the dog's mind? Why do I tell you this? I know many couples treat their dog as their firstborn, like a practice round for children. Their firstborn dog-child is an integral part of the family who needs some guidance in the adjustment too. I suggest (in jest) that the Doberman perceived the loss of the couple's attention—previously focused on him—and suffered PPMD. Brief, but extreme. As mentioned, PPMD is unpredictable. You can add your granddog to your list of who needs your caring ways.

Grandmother: listen, hold baby, love baby as well as the rest of the family. Help support the mother in getting sleep, good nutrition, and time off duty and out of earshot of baby. For a mother who wakes up Monday morning with no sign of being off duty for a week or longer, it's already a blue day. Identify specifics of what she is doing well and include words like "You're a good mom" and a compliment about baby.

My aunt taught her child to tell any approaching mom with a carriage that her baby is beautiful because mothers like to hear that. Instead of putting unrealistic expectations on yourself or telling others to be strong, just BE. Remind everyone of inner strengths. Despite your best efforts, your mere proximity may make you the target of anger or grief. Endeavour to not take it personally.

A powerful Hawaiian heart healing practice is *Ho'oponopono**—loosely meaning "make it right"—and this can be done for yourself as well as for others to get rid of negative feelings. You can do it without the other person knowing, and a dramatic positive shift can happen with witnesses confused as to what transpired when the complainer turns pleasant.

The four steps are saying aloud,

Repentance: "I'm sorry."

Forgiveness: "Forgive me."

Gratitude: "Thank you."

Love: "I love you."

If you are ever at a loss for words, say these: "Let there be peace."

Realize that each of us is a work in progress, as well as a miracle in motion. Patience is a virtue.

How will you move beyond differences with your grandbaby's mother so you can, together as well as separately, put baby's well-being as top priority? Savour the beautiful moments. Expect blessings. Seek the good in everyone—including yourself—and forgive easily. Catch

---

*Publisher's Note: *Ho'oponopono* is an ancient Hawaiian spiritual practice which is based on the principles of repentance, gratitude, and responsibility for the world. While its origins are deeply rooted in profound spiritual teachings which would originally be facilitated by a revered elder of the community, it has been brought into modern day spiritual practice as a short four-line prayer which can be used by any individual as a personal healing prayer of forgiveness for self and others. Ho'oponopono can be studied as a whole spiritual healing program or simply practiced by an individual as the prayer "I love you. I'm sorry. Please forgive me. Thank you."

everyone being good at whatever they are doing. Let them know their contributions make a positive difference. Tell them they are good enough. No need for perfection or striving.

Plan the wonderful adventures you will have as a twosome and as a triad. Appreciate the joys they will have as mother and baby and can tell you about.

Your imagination has even more power than your relationship. Together, you are stronger, and every generation wins. Let her know how special she, the mother of your precious grandbaby, is.

A new mom's suggestion for grandmothers: "Make the effort to really get to know the baby and be present with the baby when visiting."

It sounds like she is describing Grammie Camp.

Guess what? Lots of triads are full of happiness.

I first watched the 1960 Disney movie *Pollyanna* in my youth. It had an immediate and lasting impact on my thinking. The story evolves as a clever father shifts his daughter's extreme disappointment to a contagious perspective of gratitude. Pollyanna's parents are poor missionaries and she had asked the mission centre for a doll for Christmas. She had never had a doll of her own and is crushed when, instead of a doll, she receives crutches. Those underappreciated crutches inspire the birth of the "glad game" her father creates to teach her to seek the silver lining and turn disappointment into gratitude. He explains that although she did not receive the doll, she can be glad she does not need the crutches. Later, Pollyanna's parents die, and orphaned Pollyanna is sent to live with her very wealthy, single, prominent, and politically powerful Aunt Polly who is not happy to have a child foisted upon her.

A crutch is to support a physically lame person. How many of us, though, are lame in spirit or attitude? Aunt Polly is emotionally distant to all. As it turns out, Pollyanna is a gift to many negative and reclusive town folk initially irked by Pollyanna's incessant renditions of "I'm glad that..." The original crutches morphing into the glad game miraculously serve to support the hearts and minds of many. It's how we respond to adversity, not the adversity itself that helps us grow.

So it is with Grammie Camp. Whether it's with your grandbaby or her mom, you can soften hearts and ease the challenge of unfamiliar territory. When Mom expresses inadequacy, you can remind her that baby knows her to be the best. She can be glad that she is not expected to ever know everything but to just do her best and that is enough. Be glad that experience comes from experience and that has yet to be had. The glad game can become your regular way of being, one that raises the happiness baseline for yourself and others.

What are some specific ways you can have Grammie Camp with baby and mother?

- Praise! Praise! Praise! As on an airplane, if oxygen is needed, put on your mask first. Support and encourage Mom so she, in turn, can support her baby. Practice praising with your own internal dialogue. Are you your best cheerleader or your worst critic? It's a choice.

- Notice what she is doing well. Tell her. Be specific. "I notice you hold the baby close and speak softly. That helps her feel secure. Good job!" or "I see you pull the leg ruffles out when diapering. That will save you some laundry. Aren't you clever?" or "I see the baby's body relax when you sing and rock her." or "I am impressed that you take baby out for a walk, even when it's cold. Have you noticed she sleeps better after the fresh air?"

- Protect Mom's sleep. Identify with her. Say things like "Sleep deprivation is so difficult" or "I am so impressed with you. What do you do that helps you?"

- Judge not. One mother solo parenting by plan rationalized her lack of help with the lack of need to attend to a partner's feelings about their own wants or opinions. Many women who desire children, yet lack a suitable partner, choose to have a baby.

Despite entering motherhood "with eyes wide open"—if that is possible—there is no escape from the shock of how intense and all-consuming it is. Male couples with a surrogate may have a smaller peer support group of co-fathering but the highs and lows of parenting apply regardless. Life is always miraculous.

- Encourage her to put her phone on silent. No need to respond ASAP just because someone calls. No one wants to awaken a sleeping mom or a breastfeeding learning session. Breastfeeding is a six-week learning process with ups and downs, so an uninvited audience is not conducive to calm.

- Bring meals or make them while there with planned surplus and do the cleanup.

- Hold baby so her parents can sit down and eat a hot meal.

- During feedings, offer Mom liquids. After breastfeeding, offer to burp and settle baby. If bottle fed, offer to do the feeding. If acceptable to Mom, let baby sleep in your arms. Sleep usually lasts longer. Babies do prefer to be with a human rather than be alone in a still, silent, cool container. Not every culture separates mother and baby.

- Offer Mom a back massage in her bed so she can happily drift off to sleep.

- Take baby outdoors for a walk so any crying is out of earshot of mom, and she is emotionally off duty.

- Offer to stay home with baby so mom can go for a walk solo or with her dog or partner, as they did pre-parenthood.

- Tell her she made a beautiful baby, and you are so proud of her adjustment to motherhood.

- Ask Mom, "How can I be helpful?" She may rattle off a long list or direct you to a list on the fridge (I suggest that in prenatal class). As you or Mom think of ways you or other visitors can help, those ideas can be added, much like a grocery list: vacuum, laundry, dishes, pick up groceries, mail, etc.

- Ask Mom, "What's working well for you?" It's not always easy to recognize the good stuff.

- Take pictures of Mom shining in her new role.

- Just keep Mom company. She may crave adult company, whether conversation or just presence.

- Be a good listener to complaints such as sore breasts or sleep deprivation. Don't say, "I know exactly how you feel" because you don't. Be intentional about paying attention. To nurture Mom first-hand is to nurture baby second-hand.

- Use your experience to cope with a crying baby. Don't give her back as soon as she cries. Parents need a break.

- Take baby out in dark night air. Listen to the sounds of the night.

- Sing to baby. Whistle. Hum. Yodel. Talking is only one form of vocalization. Be yourself and share your talents.

- Share aloud what you think baby is feeling (or what Mom or Dad may want to hear). "Thanks, Mom." or "Isn't Daddy clever to know you need a diaper change?" or tell baby about when her mom was a baby. "She liked this song." Stick with the good stuff.

- Empathize with challenges of navigating this foreign parenting journey. After my first baby, I recall saying at about one month, "I think I'm getting the hang of this." Then, at two months, "*Now* I feel comfortable in my new role," which continued for months. Experience comes with experience!

- Be flexible about which side of the family gets to host baby's first Thanksgiving, birthday, etc.

- Be supportive of how Mom chooses to parent.

- Take "should" out of your vocabulary.

- Practice understanding your own feelings.

Getting comfortable driving with a baby in the car is a learning curve, so the following may also be helpful:

- Accompany Mom and baby on short drives to build confidence. Sit in back seat with baby so Mom can focus more on driving.
- Go with Mom to doctor appointments for reassurance and an extra pair of hands to hold baby so she can be attentive to conversation with the doctor.

There are also some cautions or don'ts.

- Don't take over. Otherwise, the message is: "I know how, and you don't."
- Don't give advice unless asked. Even then, help her figure it out and realize she can.
- Don't criticize. Her fledgling confidence will be hypervigilant and sensitive to any hint of inadequacy.
- Don't just settle into the home. Respect privacy and family cocooning.
- Don't push her to sleep if what she wants to do is check emails or chat with a friend. Sometimes a change is as good as a rest.
- Don't ask how you can help, then decline to do what is requested.
- Don't worry. Worry is like praying for what you don't want to happen. It's also contagious and not helpful to anybody. Worry or fear is the opposite of faith, and you want the mom to believe that you believe in her ability to be a good mother (which, of course, you tell her often).

Expect success. Forget the past. Don't worry about the future. Enjoy the moment. Enjoy your grandbaby. In truth, whether you are mother or in-law or an aunt with a special name, your biggest challenge is to be deemed an asset and an ego-builder. Once you have become those, you will be welcome, and when you are welcome, your role will be all the richer.

You may notice baby's mother is watching you two in action, purposefully learning about life and love and the joy of learning. Mom can watch, then happily go off to her own activities with a smile on her face, knowing she is part of a great team and that her baby is lucky indeed.

The triad's centre is the mother. The triad will triumph when you honour her in that position. Arm her with as much love as possible. The more you show you trust her and believe in her, the more she can rely on herself to care for her baby and not lean on you to figure things out. You can evolve baby-care strategies *with* her, not *for* her. Then she can give birth anew to her emerging and ever-evolving confidence as a mother.

The triad will triumph in a three-way street with love and learning between baby, mother, and grandmother, and that will be conducive to each of you thriving independently and together.

A Letter from Grandbaby

Dear Coco,

I am glad you and Mommy are friends. When I grow up, I want to still go for picnics with both of you. Do you think if I get a brother, he will do dad and grampa picnics instead of with us?

Mommy said she loved you giving her a back massage. I like it too when you put coconut oil on my skin after a bath. How did you get to be so smart? I don't know who loves me more, you or Mommy.

See you next time, Coco.

Kisses from me,

Katie

Every mama needs self-care and TLC.

All water bodies can be fun for baby.

Four generations of first borns: baby, Mama, Nana, and Grandma

Four generations together and captured for posterity.

Adventures in the outdoors stimulate all of baby's senses.

Fur mamas and new babies bond too.

Chapter 5
Communication Cues

Babies come with their own language, their own way of telling you, non-verbally, what they feel and want.

"Keys to Infant Caregiving. Infant Cues."
Parent-child Relationship Programs at the Barnard Center

You have wisdom gleaned from life experience and knowledge that incorporates baby-nurturing skills you may not have needed to tap into until you became a grandmother. You have innumerable inner resources, and you may find this chapter reinforces what you already know. You have much power and influence to make a significant impact on your infant grandchild's health and happiness. You concurrently can increase your own happiness and the world's, one grandmother and baby at a time. You might imagine yourself as birthing a new contribution to the world. Share your brilliance and joys of your version of Grammie Camp because it will be unique.

It has been said that smiling is the universal language. Wait, a newborn doesn't smile yet. Hmm...better learn how else this new person communicates. Personally, I do believe newborn babies smile. My midwife and I both witnessed my baby smile at two days old. I don't smile when I have gas, so why would my baby? A baby can smile awake or asleep, so perhaps it's related to all systems being immature and smiling out the kinks. Although it may not be intentional or the result of pleasure or joy, it is a smile. At about three or four weeks, though, a baby who is smiled at learns to smile back.

If you think learning a newborn or infant's communication is challenging, imagine how baby finds learning *your* language. Fortunately, it's a learnable skill, achieved by the interested parties. If the need persists, a solution will be found. By adulthood, we have learned to guard our emotions and thoughts. Many, if not all, of us still have feelings of "not good enough" or "not lovable," or we rely on external factors to make us feel worthy. This could be through academic success, status, career, a fancy car, a showpiece partner, material wealth, or others' opinions of us. On the other hand, a baby's physiology is regulated externally. He is dependent on a trusted caregiver for nutrition and temperature control, as well as meeting physical and emotional needs.

With your Grammie Power, you can groom your grandbaby's feeling of being more than enough, being worthy, being lovable and loved, and being important, seen, and heard.

Crying is a baby's number-one communication tool. Body language is second, and words come later. So, *observe* to see what baby is telling you. Guess, even if your first guess may not be correct. *Listen* and hear the subtleties in vocalization. A baby's state of wakefulness and engagement/disengagement cues are sent both audibly and physically. Your job is to figure them out. There are great resources to help.

My favourite teaching tool for mothers on my home visits as a community health nurse is called "Baby Cues:® A Child's First Language." It's a boxed deck of cards bearing photographs with babies on one side and flip-side notes on what baby might be communicating and how you can help. So many of the mothers I guided in early parenting had no experience with babies until they had their own and had no idea how to "read" their baby. These cards were used on repeated visits as mothers learned to understand their babies and gained confidence in themselves as mothers.

No one is born knowing, and many isolated moms have no one to watch and learn from. To add to a sense of inadequacy in this new job—the most important ever—many women who are accustomed to being competent in their jobs or careers have a tough time feeling out of their league and having to ask questions and thereby demonstrating their lack of expertise. Many moms who are excited to learn have told me, "I wish my parents had played with me. I have no idea how to play with my baby." More broadly, they may have wished they'd been around more people who played with their babies to have learned by observing.

No play is without purpose. Having fun is purpose, but a baby's curiosity finds interest in both the novel element and the familiar or favourites that build a sense of mastery. The primary learning mechanism of humans is observation, so observe!

Remember, all babies are unique, just as grandmothers are. Learn to appreciate uniqueness and, most importantly, learn baby's language. There will be times you have no idea why baby is crying, despite using all the usual successful strategies. Baby may not know either! Yet, at some point, crying stops. Believe that your soothing attempts are valuable, nonetheless. If you were upset and your friend said, "Stop being upset" or "Just go to sleep," would you feel valued? Sometimes misery needs company in the form of someone demonstrating an effort to alleviate the issue. Intention and action count, even if the desired outcome doesn't seem obvious.

Pediatrician Dr. T. Berry Brazelton noted in his 2006 book, *Touchpoints, Birth to Three: Your Child's Behavioral and Emotional Development*, that the outcome of cues sent to him is reliant on baby's ability to receive, to integrate, and to respond to those cues. If we stress and show disappointment in baby not achieving, a worse risk is damage to his self-esteem. When baby shows excitement in his own success, his self-esteem is okay. This doctor sees both the baby and the parent perspective.

For example, a nine-month-old can seem out of control and parents don't know why. Dr. Brazelton empathizes and directs them to baby's viewpoint. When working on new skills, such as crawling or standing, some disorganization is created, and that likely spills over into sleep and feeding. The challenge is in the upheaval. The lesson is that periods of regression usually precede leaps in progression. Grammie Camp is unlikely to be exempt from this natural rhythm, so go with the flow.

Can you spoil a baby? No! When an adult responds to baby's needs, this helps develop self-regulation. Can a baby manipulate you? No! An older child, yes, but if that child has learned his needs will be met, he won't need to manipulate. It's a good investment on so many levels.

In 1946, Dr. Benjamin Spock, M.D., American pediatrician, wrote a wildly popular and broadly relied upon book called *The Common Sense Book of Baby and Child Care* that sold half a million copies in the six months after publication. By the time he died in 1998, fifty million had been sold. Spock encouraged parents to trust their instincts, their own common sense, and told parents that they know more than they think they do. He advocated treating babies as individuals, not as mini-adults, but with total respect between children and adults. He did not approve of constant strict discipline, but promoted parents treating children as individuals, showing love and affection to their children. This was a huge departure from prior parenting advisers who said this would make for weaker children.

I met Dr. Spock in the hallway at a parenting conference in perhaps 1977. I don't remember exactly what we discussed, but I was impressed with his fervent beliefs. As stated earlier in the Triad Triumphs chapter, we may not always remember what a person said, but we do remember how that person made us feel. As a young, impressionable nurse, it was good to hear a famed parenting aficionado unabashedly speaking his truth, rethinking his truth at the conference, and showing that I was worthy of an impromptu conversation. Perhaps it was an epiphany of the day for both of us. So, it is with your grandmothering role. Give yourself permission as you learn to change your ideas and beliefs as you grow.

Temperament is something we are born with. Yours may be quite different from your grandbaby's. He may appreciate quiet and calm, while you revel in loud and busy. Allow baby to gently and leisurely get comfortable, with you nearby, because security breeds self-confidence. Babies need personal space too. A stranger's face and voice suddenly poking into the stroller to gush over baby can be enough reason for crying and seeking rescue.

Try something once. If right, baby will show that's what he likes. You soon will know his preferences.

By identifying baby's state of arousal, you can plan what to do during those shifts. They are:

- CRYING—Babies cry for several reasons: wet, dry, hungry, overstimulated, bored, too hot or cold, discomfort/pain, lonely, afraid, startled, or any number of unidentified reasons. Engagement during the crying state may be limited while trying all the approaches to soothing of the stated reasons. Very little can be accomplished for baby while in such distress.

- ACTIVE, ALERT—Babies are comfortable, awake, energetic, and at their best to meet you for interactions and new experiences.

- QUIET, ALERT—Babies are also comfortable yet in a more subdued way. Reading, talking, singing, and other low energy interactions are best during this time.

- DROWSY—Babies are showing signs of disconnect, lethargy, and tiredness. It may be best to soothe and ease them into sleep rather than rousing them; they may rebel by crying.

- ACTIVE OR LIGHT SLEEP—Babies may be hovering just between wakefulness and sleepy time. During this time, they may startle easily into alertness, or may wake if sounds or positions shift. So, it is not the time for interactions.

- QUIET OR DEEP SLEEP—This is the restful rejuvenating state in which even the television or phone doesn't interrupt. This is the time for Grandma to either also take a break or offer to help Mom with some of the earlier suggestions. Ahh, so sweet is the sight of a sleeping baby.

Timing is everything. Sleepy time is not the time to introduce new, interesting experiences (even if that was your plan). Active, alert time is not the time to focus on getting baby to sleep, even if it's because you are the tired one. An exercise in futility serves no one. Baby is not watching the clock. So rather than your watching the clock, focus on messages baby is giving, not the ones you are hoping for.

As you follow baby's curiosity, observe what appeals to him. What is he noticing? Is there a need or a way to distract or capitalize on what he is communicating? If you focus on the positive, more will come your way. If you expect and project gloom, it will come your way. Invest good thoughts and actions in your grandbaby, ones that you would appreciate for yourself. Celebrate your own efforts. Generate fun, joy, and happiness, and you both win. The family circle—and the ever-growing community that baby is a part of—all win with an engaged, secure baby/child/adult. That's Grammie Power! To foster anyone's imagination and zest for learning is a valuable gift.

You can help by learning baby's cues and acting on them, monitoring his response to environmental stimuli, such as noise, lighting, temperature, and rituals to indicate sleep time and feeding time. So many baby communication cues are the same for adults, but we don't pay attention the same way once we rely on words. As the grandmother of a baby, the most important language you need to hone is body language. Looking interested or away, engaging in conversation or being distant, and leaving or staying in the room all provide signals we may be unaware of; we may not understand yet may be offended and continue our own exhausting inner dialogue about our flaws, instead of asking the person for clarification. Their communication with you may be related to their own ruminating over an issue unrelated to you. If in doubt, check it out. Rely on your inner cheerleader instead of inner critic. That is also a learnable skill you can teach your grandbaby once you have learned it.

It may help to put yourself in baby's shoes and imagine how he might feel in any given moment. At the end of a typically busy day, you too might not know what to do with yourself. If nothing has happened all the boring day, you might fuss to create some action too.

In addition to the impact of baby's state of wakefulness and sleep, you need to learn his engagement and disengagement cues. They are body language or baby signals in place of words. Some are obvious, saying "More!" and some more subtly saying, "Not now. I need a time out. I don't like what's happening." Even when having fun, a baby will reach a saturation point. Peekaboo is fun, but not for an hour at a time. Likewise, you both may enjoy tickling and giggling, but it can also be exhausting. Don't take a disengagement cue personally. A break is in order at some point. You will learn to read your baby's cues by observing with curiosity.

Some *engagement* cues are movements and sounds from baby indicating interest in the activity offered: smiling, eyes wide and bright, raising head to look toward you, open hands, trying to touch or taste, reaching toward you or a toy, snuggling in, relaxed body, crawling to you, and babbling. When baby is relaxed in your arms, he is saying, "I am secure with you."

Some *disengagement* cues include turning head or body away (from you or spoon, if being fed), pounding surface or throwing things, arching back, stiffness, body thrashing (especially if you don't seem to be getting the message), irregular breathing, skin growing pale or red or mottled, frowning, pouting, yawning, hands to mouth or ear, fingers open wide, crying, spitting, gagging, kicking, hiccups/cough/sneeze, dull-looking eyes (like at half-mast), or going to sleep. Notice there are so many more disengagement cues. Surely you will recognize enough to change what's happening, and baby will feel understood.

In our eons-old survival mechanism, we are wired to notice the negative, the potential threat. Though we are unlikely to need to run from being prey, it's still in us to flee. That sets up a fight or flight response that bathes us in cortisol, which serves the urgency, if there is one, but does a disservice if the stress response of a chemical dump lingers. Though you may not be able to teach baby relaxed breathing, you can do it, and he can relax in seeing your relaxed face and feeling your body relax.

As a grandmother, you may have the luxury of more time to learn relaxation and mindfulness techniques to keep the disease-inducing cortisol at bay. Grandparenting and supporting adults who feel unprepared for parenting *is* stressful. When that situation occurs, having your own practised relaxed breathing can ease the anxiety. Nasal breathing releases nitric oxide, which dilates blood vessels, has a calming effect and gets more oxygen to the muscles. Everything in the body works better with good oxygen flow.

Sometimes grandmothers are thrust into a parenting role for a variety of reasons, often a parent's mental health. Even so-called cognitively low-functioning moms can be taught to nurture babies when motivated. Attachment theory is still greatly researched, with many intervention programs being developed.

A famous 1975 research experiment called the "Still Face Experiment," by Dr. Edward Tronick, a developmental psychologist at the Gottman Institute, noted infants need emotional connection early in life and are responsive to external stimuli. In his experiment, a mother and a baby are interacting playfully, face-to-face, with the baby in a highchair. Then the mother is instructed to look at the baby and not respond but to have a "still face" for two minutes. The baby becomes very distressed, trying to elicit a response in the usual ways. It can be distressing just to watch the video. Next, the mother is asked to resume usual responding to the baby's cues, and the baby is quickly content.

If ignoring is the dominant caregiver style, baby's resilience may be severely challenged.

Put yourself in baby's place and imagine your best friend and you are enjoying an animated discussion that is truncated by two minutes of her inexplicable silence. She then resumes the conversation, as if all is normal, and offers no explanation. In the experiment, the baby showed resilience and recovery from the two-minute abrupt shift in response. However, ongoing lack of response can damage his mental health. How does he feel loved and secure when his caregiver shifts from present to distant in a moment? How does an orphan cope with a hired caretaker's indifference as opposed to at least one predictable care*giver*? When the adult is unaware of baby's need for an expressive caregiver, baby may receive excellent physical care as the caregiver awaits infant's or child's readiness or being "old enough" to connect. The potential downfall is as the caregiver gives little feedback, baby waits and waits, watching for something—anything—and may eventually give up or appear depressed.

Attachment theory was famously studied by psychologist and psychiatrist John Bowlby in 1969, regarding the need for infants to form an attachment bond of trust with at least one caregiver. Absence of that attachment through separation or fear (physical, verbal, or sexual abuse) or not knowing its importance due the caregiver's own emotional lack (severe depression or anxiety) were all deemed problematic for baby's development. Bowlby believed if this attachment was not developed in the first two and a half years, it was a lost opportunity and future relationships would be fraught with the inability to form lasting trusting relationships later in life.

We are born not knowing anything about ourselves or the world in relation to us. Our beliefs in adult life stem from early childhood messages primarily at home and mostly from parents. If an infant falls or is sick and adult response is one of uncaring, unkind, or even a nonresponse, baby may assign a meaning to the fall or ailment that he is unimportant or not lovable. So begins an unconscious limiting belief. In contrast, when he receives words or actions of love and caring, he feels loved and lovable. These different fledgling beliefs have lasting impact. In fact, the event has no meaning until our mind interprets it and concludes it is negative or positive, while there could be other interpretations equally valid. The event may not have been noticed or the adult's own belief may be to let the infant cry, so he doesn't get spoiled. We need to be ever mindful of the full spectrum of our communication. It's one of those things in life that is simple yet not easy.

Grammie Camp is purposeful interacting with obvious interest in baby's communication through saying, doing, or crying and incorporating facial or body cues. Grammie's role is to be the reliable support, to validate emotions, to soothe and give attention that lets baby know you enjoy him. Give him breaks and space to rest, then recharge and reconnect when ready. When we have time apart, we appreciate the time back together as refreshing, instead of being too much of a good thing.

Who are the fastest learners on the planet? Children, once they ask questions. They quickly learn the most useful word is *Why?* Before being verbal, your grandbaby still asks this *why* when he frowns quizzically in response to something unusual. His natural curiosity and wonder can rekindle yours with reciprocal awe in the world's offerings. It is okay to say you don't know the answer to something and that you're going to try to find out and let him know. If you don't perceive a question, you need not seek an answer. Grandmothers can help grandmothers learn, as can babies and grandbabies inspire the need to learn. To foster anyone's imagination and zest for learning is a worthwhile endeavour.

In good communication, what isn't said is just as significant as what is. Make educated guesses and try to affirm them but make no assumptions. With the goal of Grammie Camp being to seek, create, and observe opportunities to have intentional activities and interactions with grandbaby, it is crucial to learn infant communication cues.

Patterns learned early in life tend to be perpetuated into adulthood unless reason, inclination, and determination to communicate differently are present. It is easier to learn both sending and receiving styles of messaging than to relearn, it seems. Words do matter. Semantics are important. Intonation and volume also need to match the words. If you say, "I love you," but your face and body suggest otherwise, the ambiguous message makes it difficult to interpret.

I recall a story of a grade one teacher berating the students. An astute six-year-old asked the teacher why she didn't like children. Horrified, she defended herself saying, "I love children. They are my joy." The child said, "Well, will you tell your face what your mouth just said?" If we listen to our young critics, we may learn surprising things about ourselves. Though we associate the word *abracadabra* with pulling a rabbit out of a hat, Hebrew roots translate it as "I will create as I speak." The word's Aramaic roots mean, "I create like the word." So, when you use words to, about, or within hearing range of baby, use words that give life, optimism, and positive vibrations.

We are about 70 percent water, and even water crystals respond to positive and negative words. Dr. Masaru Emoto published microscopic photographs of water that had received very different input and treatment. Children spoke differently to the water in the jars. Some jars received loving words, others, hateful ones. Some jars of water received soothing music, while others were played harsh, loud music. The water appeared to respond to these differences. Once frozen, the water crystals ranged from unattractive blobs to exquisite patterns. The very organized and beautiful crystals were the ones reacting to positive words and sounds. Unattractive crystals formed in reaction to the negative input. I notice a similar effect in facial expressions of people at rest. I recall in high school determining to smile often so my older face later would not be of a scowl or bulldog look. Catching a glimpse of oneself in a mirror or store window can be revealing of what others see on our faces. We hope they make no assumptions! Our degree of hydration as well as our thoughts and emotions affect our wrinkles or puffiness or at-rest expression. This water research continues and invites the study of environmental impact on our water content that is so much a part of us. Being largely water, we are also impacted by words and emotions.

Perhaps an unpleasant facial demeanour reflects unkind self-talk or external negativity.

A baby understands much before he can verbalize it. His receptive language develops before his expressive language. Most babies can begin to learn signing with their hands between eight and twelve months old. They make hand gestures to indicate their needs, like wanting milk. This is different from American Sign Language, and of course you need to learn it so you can teach it. There are books and classes to learn sign language, if desired. Signing is not necessary but is an option. An obvious sign, perhaps not thought of as such, is clapping, which can be learned around nine months and is a commonly expressed joy in cheerleading and celebrating with baby. Another sign is waving bye-bye and reaching their arms out to be picked up. See? Sign language is already a part of your life.

Praising baby often as an ongoing series of small wins has more impact than simply one large win. A whole year of wins celebrated along the way by you and others surpasses a single huge one-year-old birthday bash. Celebrate wins as they occur, likely every day. Set baby up for wins. As adults, we track meals, sleep, miles, and exercises. For all of us at every age, one of the best things to track is wins!

Ways to include communication cues in Grammie Camp include:

- Be curious. You can ask, "I wonder what you would like to do now?" or "Ah, your eyes look sleepy. Let's read a book, then you can have a little nap."

- Stop. Look. Listen. What is baby telling you?

- Be playful.

- Track wins. Every little one you can. Cheer in the moment. Recount the win. Capture it on camera. Relive all the good stuff. To repeat is to reinforce so let go of the non-wins except to learn from them.

- Use variety in communication.

- *Allow* baby to try something new. Don't insist.

- Incorporate what lights you up and notice whether this also appeals to baby. If not, what does? Ask yourself: How can I make this fun?

- Communicate in a variety of ways that you love him. Keep blessing him with your goodness!

A Letter from Grandbaby

Dear Granny,

I am glad you figured out my kissing action means "yes." I sure wish I could speak like you. I do love all the songs and bath time. My muscles work so hard. I am glad you cool me down with a soothing voice as you pray, drizzle water, and just love me. Although I don't have the words to express it, I hope you know, I love you a whole lot!

Love,

Jack

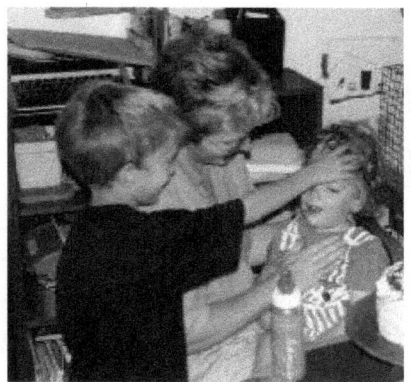

God Bless the Children

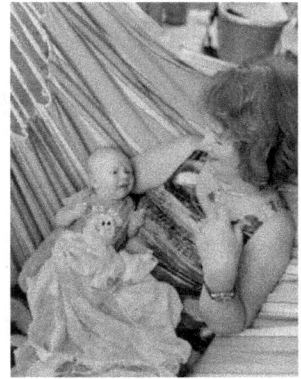

Position baby for seeing and responding to faces.

New baby and Mom, practicing focus.

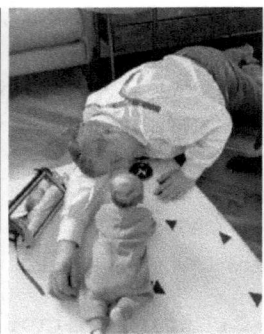

Mosom and nosisim sharing love of books.

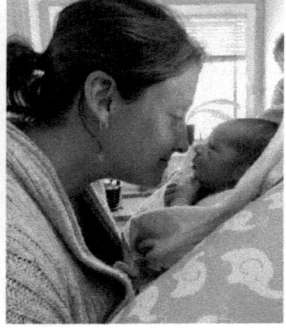

Baby and Mom appreciatively studying each other.

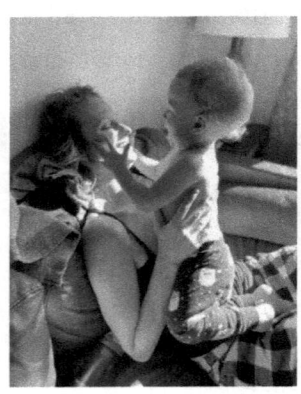

Touch, see, and hear me.

Family resemblance between father and son.

Twins creating their special language.

Chapter 6
Grandmothers Share Wisdom

A wise woman does not keep her wisdom to herself. She shares wisdom with the world because she knows that through wisdom, many lives can be transformed.

Gift Gugu Mona, Woman of Virtue: Power-Filled Quotes for a Powerful Woman

---

Do you consider yourself wise? Do you consider yourself knowledgeable? Although these two descriptors are related, they are not synonymous. After a few (or several) decades of life, you are both. One definition of wisdom is the ability to discern or judge what is true, right, or lasting. Being knowledgeable on a subject is being well-informed. Knowledge understands your grandbaby learns through putting things in her mouth. Wisdom says that if it is not safe to be in baby's mouth, have it out of baby's sight or reach. Knowledge says your grandbaby is naturally curious. Wisdom says to provide varied, fun learning opportunities in a safe environment.

"When the student is ready, the teacher appears" is one of the basics of Grammie Camp. You initially are the motivated student to learn your baby's communication cues (her language). Then you appear as the teacher to interact in ways conducive to her feeling valued and learning how to be in her world. Like common sense, wisdom is not doled out in equal portions. It is earned by reflecting on experience. You gain knowledge and learn to apply it wisely.

Let's assume you are wise.

In gathering opinions of grandmothers both formally and informally through a survey, grandmothers were asked what three non-material gifts they hope to impart to their grandbabies. It's interesting that of the many specified values, three themes were evident, and they were by number of respondents, given comparable priority. Not surprisingly, grandmothers want these babies to have it all.

Although only one specified "my time," let's assume its importance is inherent in achieving each of the values. Some grandmothers clearly were thinking beyond baby's first year, which is natural because most of us spend more thought lost in the past (What did I learn or not learn up until now?) or the future (How will she turn out as an adult?) than in the present.

For Grammie Camp, you need to be *in* the present and literally *be present*. Be kind to yourself in this learning process. Developing good communication with another human being takes time. As you learn baby's engagement and disengagement cues (see Chapter 5), you will realize those same cues are also expressed by adults, so the knowledge is beneficial outside Grammie Camp as well. The more you respond lovingly and accurately to baby's cues, the more she learns to read you, and so goes the give and take of two-way communication. What's rewarded is repeated.

The one hundred and fifty grandmothers I surveyed have grand aspirations for values they hope to impart through communication with their grandbabies. In order of frequency, the top three equally mentioned are:

- LOVE: Loving, feeling loved and lovable, knowing what love is, love for self, others, animals, and nature.

- COMPASSION: Empathy, acceptance, tolerance, inclusiveness.

- KINDNESS: Being kind to others and expecting kindness from them.

Values mentioned next most frequently fit into the following groupings:

- IMAGINATION: Curiosity and love of learning.

- HAPPINESS: Joy, laughter, fun loving.

- FAMILY: Value of time together, traditions, heritage.

- ADVENTURES: Love of exploring outdoors; moon watching, observing the seasons and what they offer: snow, blooms/blossoms, harvest, leaves.

- CREATIVITY: Love of creating music, painting, baking, gardening.

Personal skills and character traits hoped for were: importance of faith, strong work ethic, and pursuit of excellence, confidence, courage, and determination.

In addition to values, other questions were about skills, attributes, and hopes for the future.

- Personal attributes identified included: honesty, patience, strength, feeling special/self-worth/self-confidence, ability to identify and acknowledge own unique gifts and strengths, and expression of talent in sports and arts.

- Family values included: listen to parents, respect family history, stay connected.

- Community connections included: being a good person, tolerant, non-judgmental, sharing, being charitable.
- Future hopes included: self-sufficiency, courage to follow own path, belief that anything is possible, trust that the universe is benevolent, and enjoy and feel present in life's moments.

People skills also made the list.

- Energetic connection. Safe, open communication (with Grammie too!)
- Ability to connect with others.
- Importance of friends. Memories. Everlasting love.
- Lend a hand. Help people in need. Kindness and consideration of others.
- Forgive others for wrongs. It is not condoning their actions, but it is freeing you from ruminating. Be at peace.
- Forgive yourself for mistakes. We can learn with each one.

As you see, grandmothers have high hopes for their grandbabies.

What are your personal values? How will you teach and model these to your grandbaby? Who else can you involve? What will your legacy be? Your *personal* legacy of benevolent values serves a higher purpose than gifts of money or property can.

What grandmothers want for their grandbabies is often what they also want (or wish they'd had) for themselves. Notably, no one expressed desire to spare the infant all discomforts, fears, or ailments. These are natural and inevitable elements of life that groom us for whatever purpose we have on Earth.

Grammie Camp is an investment of time, talent, and your personal treasure that lays the groundwork to arm baby for adversity, and the gift of learning that comes with unexpected outcomes. Your role is to do your best in a loving manner, to demonstrate, live, and teach your values.

In Cub Scouts, a motto rhymed off by a pack of cubs in a circle declares, "DYB DYB DYB. DOB DOB DOB." If you didn't know, you wouldn't guess what it means.

Do Your Best. Do Your Best. Do Your Best.

Do Our Best. Do Our Best. Do Our Best.

Part of your Grammie Camp plan would do well to incorporate that message. When you do your best, your grandbaby has the inspiration to do her best.

Here are some specific ways to share your values with your grandbaby.

How do you show you value adventures?

- Go for walks in forests to let baby know you enjoy the outdoors.
- Bundle up for cool fall walks and teach that any day or weather is good to go out.
- Focus on baby while out in carriage. Position baby to see your face as well as the view, not just the inside of the top of the carriage. Stay off your phone. Keep your attention on baby and your surroundings.
- Expose her to unfamiliar sounds. Reassure her that you like the thunder. Be close when she is unsure about new situations. You build her confidence and calm state by being that way when with her.

How do you show you value arts and education?

- Play different genres of music. Notice her reaction. Hold her and dance to help her learn a variety of rhythms. Play percussion instruments. Use a spoon on a container to make sounds. Provide a rubber spatula to chew on, bang with, and wield with power.
- Take her to an aquarium. Fish in a tank of any size (home-size or floor-to-ceiling) are fascinating.

- Read books aloud, holding baby to see your face and the book. Let her hold, mouth, turn book around, turn page before you are ready. Follow her lead. Plastic and durable board books help.

How do you teach compassion?

- Comfort her when she is hurt, upset, or sick.
- Express concern if anyone is in emotional need.
- Take baby's hand to show how to be compassionate, like pat cat and praise: "Gentle. Kitty likes that."

How do you teach people skills?

- Spend time with people, talk, laugh. Be with people of all ages. Guard baby from uninvited closeness or loudness. Again, read her communication cues and talk as if she understands, even before she talks.
- Don't use baby talk. A baby will do that while learning your adult language.
- Don't use any words you wouldn't want baby to use.
- Sing songs. Make up songs to include baby's name.
- Talk, talk, talk, and read, read, read. Use whatever languages you know. Exposing her to different languages helps her develop an ear for later ease of learning. At birth, a baby is wired to learn any language. Once playing with other children, she will learn which one is appropriate.
- Be animated in your voice and face.
- Narrate what she is doing. To learn language, baby needs to hear it.
- Take her on tours of the house, yard, and neighbourhood, and talk about what you are seeing.
- Sit her on your lap at mealtime, even when she is not eating solids yet. She will learn the value of conversation that

accompanies eating. Plus, babies always seem to know, regardless of time, that you are about to have a meal and suddenly will need your attention. Let her join you.

- Smile often, especially when baby is in an alert state.

As you go about your day with your grandbaby, your values are lived and demonstrated. Perhaps sit down and write out the values that are important to you and strategies to make them obvious in your life. You may well find you develop new or additional values or decide some are no longer serving you or anyone else. You can always reinvent yourself. If something feels right and has a desirable outcome, do more of it. If not, let it go.

Remember, you are not babysitting when you spend time with your grandbaby. You are helping develop a loved, lovable, and loving human being with unlimited potential. Take this seriously by having a large portion of fun. Power grandmothers share themselves and their gifts, not only with grandbabies but with other grandmothers. We all benefit from a peer group who can mentor, cheerlead, and exchange ideas that one may deem basic and another brilliant.

When you were mother of a young child, perhaps mothers gathered at a home or the park so children could play together. Nowadays, it's been formalized to having (and booking) a "playdate." So be fashionable and initiate a Grammie-led playdate. Perhaps more for the grandmothers than the infants, outdoors is preferable to expand everyone's horizons, literally. A not yet crawling baby can enjoy being on a blanket and looking up to see trees dappled with sunlight, instead of a ceiling, and feel lumpy grass under the blanket. Sensory receptors delight in a banquet of sensations. Babies seem to like other babies, and grandmothers can share stories, foibles, resources, and wisdom. You may be only ten minutes from home, yet it is an adventure.

A Letter from Grandbaby

Dear Grandma,

When I was born, did I have a fairy godmother, like Cinderella did? Are you my fairy godmother? Just curious. I know you are very wise.

Love,

Lindsey

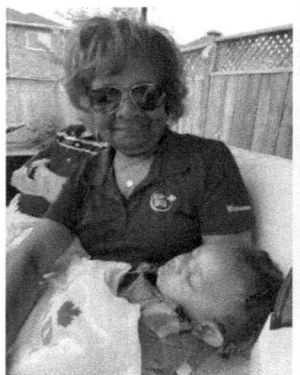

Outdoor naps for this one.

Grammie Camp philosophy says get outside often.

Great grandmas need and love contented babies too.

Grandmom shares how to smile just like her.

Grandmothers to Grandmothers, sharing wisdom and funding from Canada to Africa.

Introduction to Chapters 7 to 11
Adventures in Learning Through the Senses

> Too often we underestimate the power of a touch, a smile, a kind word, a listening ear, an honest compliment, or the smallest act of caring, all of which have the potential to turn a life around.
>
> *Leo F. Buscaglia*

Although babies are born with all five senses—hearing, sight, touch, taste, and smell—they are rudimentary and generally not operating in isolation. All are poised to take in information for baby to survive and thrive. Why is each sense given a dedicated chapter in this book? The whole is more than the sum of the parts, and by providing experiences to awaken each, your grandbaby can use Grammie Camp as a launching pad to her full potential.

Suggested activities are listed under each sense with the knowledge that any action from you may also involve other senses. External stimuli trigger baby's senses to respond in a coordinated way. With repeated exposure and ample practice, she can learn to understand her world.

Each sense has value. If one is lacking, others tend to compensate. For example, a lack of hearing may result in a heightened attunement to and reliance on visual cues and make for a better listener due to the required focus.

I recall being asked, "If you had to give up one sense, which would you choose?" That was not a conversation I wanted to pursue. I prefer to imagine or visualize a welcomed future reality because there is power in thoughts. Some say, "You are what you eat." Some say, "You are what you think." Ideally, you will nourish your grandbaby with food that's good for body, mind, heart, and soul. You too will benefit through the joy you give and receive.

People have differing dominant learning styles. A visual learner relies on seeing the information. An auditory learner needs to hear it. The kinesthetic learner needs to manipulate it. Each style works alone, but until one appears preferred, incorporate all styles. These differences are reflected in our language in sayings like, "I see what you mean. I hear what you are saying. I can see it in my mind's eye. Mothers have eyes in the back of their heads." (Did you know the eye shape of males and females differs so females can have better peripheral vision and may *seem* to see what's happening behind them?)

Be open. Relax. Believe in your ability to tap into your personal toolkit gleaned from life experiences. Observing a baby tends to invite adults to see things differently. The miracle of life evolving seems to say, "Look at me!"

Never underestimate the power of play in fostering mental health. Meditation has gained a lot of press for de-stressing but, I propose a focus on play as an adjunct or alternative. There's a saying that what's good for the goose is good for the gander. I add that it's also good for the gosling! Nature therapy could be lying awake in a stroller under a tree, mesmerized by leafy branches dancing in the breeze. Playing chase around kitchen and living room with a crawling or walking infant can have appeal akin to riding a roller coaster with fun as the surprise element versus heart-stopping fear.

Perhaps our attention is more intentional with baby. Perhaps we laugh with no inhibition when not feeling judged, as we may with an adult. Any feelings of inadequacy can be overcome by doing what seems right. Your grandbaby assumes you *know* best and *are* best. No judgment! With a relaxed you, creativity flows. With a relaxed baby, learning is easier. You both may be rookies, but you are both masterpieces worthy of prime positions in the amazing art gallery in your mind.

So much to see, hear, and feel in the breeze.

Steps in exploration and independence.

Grammie Camp says engage all the senses.

Grammie Camp philosophy: Play means everything!

Vacation adventures with Grandma.

Adventures in Learning Through the Senses

Chapter 7
Adventures in Hearing

If hearing is believing, then guard your words.

Heather Hobbs

When does your grandbaby hear? Right away, long before you first meet. While in the womb, baby heard Mom's heartbeat, digestive noises, the whoosh of placental blood, Mom's voice, and the voices of others muffled by layers of skin, fat, uterine muscle, and amniotic fluid. He can hear that loud TV, the neighbour's band, the lawnmower, arguing, singing, and being read to, sung to, and spoken to. Once baby is born, all is louder and clearer.

Babies appear to be calmed by and to enjoy white noise, such as from the clothes washer and dryer, dishwasher, vacuum, or radio static. Years ago, a young woman in the US sold cassettes with recordings of white noise, and they sold faster than she could keep up with the demand. An intrigued reporter asked her where she got such an idea. Guess who? Her grandmother! Those white noise makers and teddy bears with heartbeat sounds likely remind baby of his initial home—floating inside mom with everything provided.

The outside world is much more complicated.

By three or four months in utero, a baby can turn his head toward a sound. Just as we are affected by volume, tone, and pitch of voice, so is a baby. A stressed-out mom shares some of that stress with her baby by way of hormones, such as cortisol and adrenalin. Likewise, a calm mother shares that sense of calm via endorphins. Being at peace is good for everyone at any age.

How might your grandbaby respond to what he is hearing?

- He exhibits the "startle reflex," with all limbs extending briefly.
- He stops crying when you speak or sing or hum in soothing tones.
- He is content lying on a playmat and looking at you, but when loud, raucous music comes on, he frowns and his entire body trembles.
- He hears a loud cough and stops eating to stare at the person coughing.
- He turns toward you or parents when called by name or just spoken to.
- He smiles when you say hello.
- You cannot console him indoors so take him out into the quiet night air. He stops crying and looks around in awe.

In all these activities, you are helping your grandbaby by providing adventures in hearing. As with adults, variety is welcome. We also need repetition so we can develop mastery and anticipation.

Wield your Grammie Power through his hearing. A baby knows his mother's voice by one to three weeks of age. Given a choice of Mom's voice on one side of him and a doctor's voice on the other, he will turn his head toward Mom. Very gratifying for Mom! Research has not focused on grandmother's voice, but consistently hearing you would logically create that sense of comfort and attraction to the sound of your voice.

There are so many ways you as grandmother can enrich baby's hearing adventures.

- Use baby's name frequently. Research has shown the most important word for us to hear is our own name. It tells baby you notice him. Unless the parents approve a nickname, use his name. Baby often responds to his name by six months, though he may not say it aloud until one year or older.

- Use other people's names—the family, people on the street, on the phone. Baby will learn the face/voice connection. He will also learn others like to be called by their names.

- Tell grandbaby how he impacts you, for example, "You make me laugh." Baby's giggles start around five months and are infectious. Return the favour. Look into baby's eyes and say, "I love you. I appreciate you," or whatever you feel is relevant. Who knows at what age he understands the concept of appreciation? Start early.

- Speak as you approach your grandbaby to respond to his cries. A baby quickly learns that the sound of approaching footsteps signals help is on the way.

- Speak from your heart with caring. How special it is to witness grandbaby's face light up in response to your voice! Baby tunes in to your vibrational signature. How loud, smooth, and the quality of your voice is gradually learned as unique to you, Grandma. Baby may notice if your voice changes due to a cold, possibly frowning, as if something is amiss. Even on a video call, an atypical voice can elicit a quizzical look.

You can do some Grammie Camp preparations between visits. Make a list of songs and nursery rhymes you recall and introduce them to baby. Sing a song or record a story so it can be played for baby when you can't be there. Or contribute to a library of baby books at your home or grandbaby's. Ask early years centres or libraries about grandmother and baby classes. If none exist, request them. You are part of an underserved demographic. Of course, you can attend mom and baby classes, as can other caregivers, but having grandmother peers lends a different dimension.

Here are some Grammie Camp ideas for when you can be with grandbaby in person:

- Incorporate music with different rhythms, tempos, genres. Dance while holding baby. Support his head as you dance or bounce or support him under his arms and trunk to "fly." Jolly jumper time is greatly enhanced by music to jump to. At four to six months, he may appear to be step dancing. You can dance along.

- If you play piano, sit baby on your lap or in a front carry pack as you play. Likewise with any musical instrument, keep baby up close to feel the vibrations. Baby can hear and feel, smell the wood, touch the keys, and marvel at the clicking of the metronome. All kinds of neurons will fire in the brain to make new connections.

- Laugh when baby laughs. Make a game of laughing in different ways. Record baby's voice and play it back for him. It's true, the best medicine is joy and laughter. They are both the cause and effect of our increased flow of endorphins or happy hormones, and they boost our immunity. Silly is good!

- Hum subtly when rocking baby. The vibration becomes familiar and is comforting. A prolonged one-note hum with mouth closed is said to boost your immunity by increasing the nitric oxide, which enhances the nasal passage environment to fight pathogens. There are many books on the subject. It has a calming effect for you as well.

- When you notice something that baby enjoys, do more of it. A sense of accomplishment and security comes through repetition, and little else is under your grandbaby's control. Demonstrate that you notice what he likes.

- If sharing your faith is one of your values, speak of it. Sing spiritual songs. Go to hear church bells, organ music, and choirs singing. Read or tell faith stories.

- Speak kindly of all people. Children don't start out with prejudice. They learn it. Subliminal messaging and comments can seep through. Don't say anything about someone that you would not want to say to that person or write and sign your name to. In essence, if you wouldn't want it said about you, don't say it about anyone else.

- Speak kindly of all creatures. Don't panic at the sight of a spider and stomp on it. Call animals by their names so your grandbaby learns each identity. Listen to (and discuss) the noises those animals make.

Give your grandbaby a buffet of sounds to experience and remember to build in interludes of silence. What new sounds drift in during that quietness?

What baby needs to hear and learn and have reinforced through all his senses is to feel good about who he is, and you can become the expert on doing that.

Be a good role model compatible with all the hopes and dreams you have for this grandbaby. That's a winning goal!

A Letter from Grandbaby

Dear Kokum,

Look at that. I am speaking Cree already. Don't worry, soon you will hear me say it out loud, and I bet you will laugh and cry. You will know I am talking to my Kokum, even though all the other kids on the reserve call their grandmothers the same name. I hope every boy doesn't have my name. I was thinking about when I was four months old and getting good at laughing out loud. You are good at it too! I especially loved the time when you were singing "Old MacDonald Had a Farm," and I laughed when you sang "Cock-a-doodle-doo!" Then you laughed. We both had what you said was a good belly laugh. Someday, I hope you take me to hear a rooster that's not you. It's hard to believe the bird in my picture book can sound like you. I love when you sing and read to me. You're so much fun!

Love,

L

Find the fun in everything!

Developing ears need protection.

Chapter 8
Adventures in Sight

This is a wonderful day. I've never seen this one before.

Maya Angelou

A newborn's initial best vision is about ten to twelve inches away, perfect for face-to-face when holding baby in your arms. Within a few months, she can see you well across the room.

When you get dressed, be sure to put on a smile. Teach grandbaby this as you change her clothing. Say, "When we get dressed, we put on a smile" and smile at her. Always give baby credit for understanding more than she can tell you. Your emotional reactions can have a long-term effect on her emotional well-being.

The whole time you and your grandbaby are together, you are looking within the same space, yet from different perspectives. Consider a baby not yet able to roll over, being in one position until someone moves her. What can she see? When on her back, is there anything to look at? I found a glass coffee table perfect to lie baby under to look up at a facedown printed coaster or picture. The contrast of the coaster shape against the light through the glass would be interesting. Baby was also safe from the family dog or visiting children stepping on or falling on baby. Time on her back is a good change from sitting on a lap or in a car seat.

Tummy time can be with you seated and baby across your thighs so she can see a patterned rug or contrast between wood and tile floor. You can lie beside her on the floor or bed and sing or talk to her. If she resists turning her head to one side, make a point of engaging her briefly with a toy or you on that side so her interest in you can provide a stretch to balance the left and right side of her neck for symmetrical mobility—and to afford skull symmetry and avoid flathead. (Sometimes babies who are put to bed with their head always at the same end develop tightness as they tend to look in the direction of the doorway the caregiver comes from.)

Even for a baby with perfect vision, learning to sign such words as *milk* has a benefit before words are used. Learn, then teach these signs with baby. Later, pictures on the refrigerator such as a cup of milk can be another visual aid when words are not yet available. A combination of visual, auditory, tactile, mouthing, and smelling gives so much more information, and baby can use what works best for her.

For example, share a piece of avocado with baby. You can name it, but let baby see it, feel it, squish it, smell it, and taste it all in her own time. When you eat a piece of avocado at the same time and express positive emotions with your voice and face, she can see that people enjoy eating together.

There are so many things to do to appeal to baby's sense of sight.

- Look at each other with varying facial and body gestures.
- Play a game of "snap," changing your facial or body expression in a friendly tone.
- Look to where baby is pointing and go to or point to the same place to demonstrate your understanding of her message.

- Share a picture book and point out different elements.

- When walking, look for five things you didn't notice before. Draw baby's attention to them.

- Wear fabrics with interesting patterns and the bold colours that babies prefer over pastels.

- Notice your own gender colour coding. Do you buy a lot of pink for granddaughter and blue for grandson? There are so many colours to see and experience.

- Put baby in various positions to allow different viewpoints and sights. Tummy time, being held to look over your shoulder, and being held facing in front of you all give more options than chest to chest with you or sitting in a highchair.

- Avoid TV. A show called *Baby Einstein* is genius in marketing, but TV does not give the multi-sensory activities or feedback or relationship to a baby like Grammie does.

- Think playground, whether indoors or out. What would you like to see if you were a baby?

- Make loving eye contact. Your eyes show love and interest and curiosity. A powerful gift from a teacher—and as a grandmother, you are a teacher—is to nourish intellectual curiosity. Be a detective in seeking and deciphering baby's communication cues as she learns also to interpret yours. Try to be aware of your own communication cues.

- Be real in sharing emotions. If you have tears from grief or pain, and baby looks at you wide-eyed (as is often the response to something new and not yet understood) or quizzically or frowning, you might say, "Grammie is sad. Her friend is very sick." or "Grammie's back hurts. I can't carry you right now. Let's sit on the floor." This is a way to develop baby's emotional skills. Words saying you're fine with the idea of protecting baby or your vulnerability while your face suggests the opposite is a teachable moment lost.

- Practice looking at yourself in the mirror when you have no expression. Are you frowning? Are corners of your mouth turning up or down? Are you inviting interaction? You can start afresh in any moment. Every moment is full of potential, and your life can increase in vibrancy and joy. Your growth, though not as fast as baby's, is ongoing.

- Conserve your energy. Be attentive to your posture. Endeavour to improve your health so you will enjoy being with baby in comfort and longevity.

- Encourage baby to look at details. Look closely into the centre of a flower and encourage baby to do likewise. Also point out the trees up high. When she is in her carriage, put the hood in a position to protect baby's eyes from the sun yet give a view of the trees and clouds and buildings you pass.

- Challenge yourself to not only look but really see. Notice what you are noticing. Notice what baby may be noticing.

A Letter from Grandbaby

Dear Maa,

Our visit to the market today was amazing! So many beautiful things to see. Whether I looked up to colourful fruit stand banners or down at the tables of vegetables or sideways to other shoppers, I had so much to look at. Those cows were so funny walking in the middle of the road and so sure cars and bikes would stop for them. Thanks for the fun adventure.

Love,

Priya

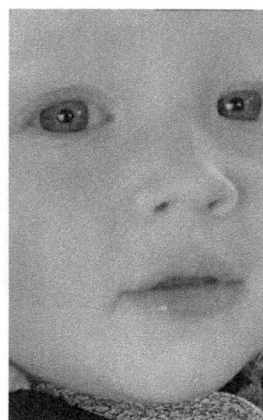
Baby gets close to explore the camera.

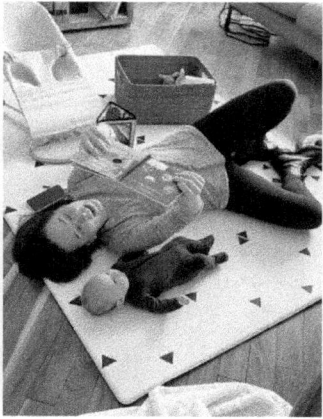
Baby loves reading anytime, anywhere.

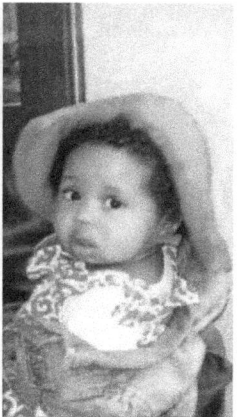
Learning to focus near and far.

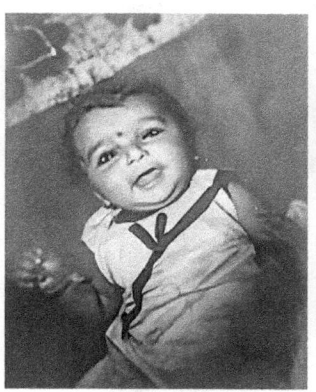
Life is beautiful.

Double vision is something to celebrate.

Sweetie playing peek-a-boo.

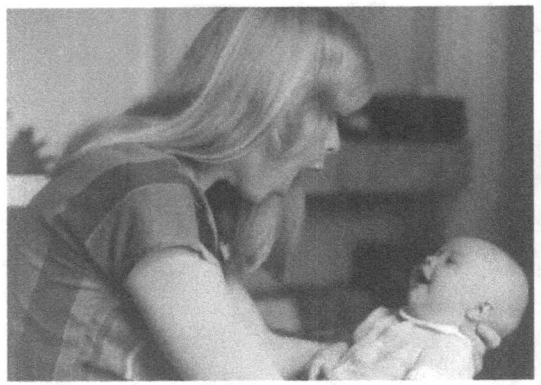
Sharing stories with Auntie of what we saw today.

Sharing Grandma.

Love at first sight and a grandma is born.

Great Grandma has seen so much more!

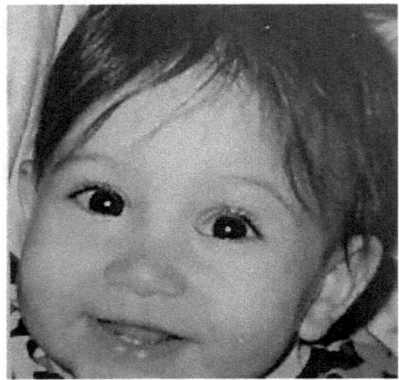
Eyes wide open to adventure.

Sharing Nana.

Chapter 9
Adventures in Touch

Touch has a memory.

John Keats

The ultimate resource is emotion. Emotions will change, and a clever grandmother is sure to focus on the positive emotions: joy, peace, and love. Touch is one way to feel these.

In utero, ultrasound indicates babies experience touch by moving away from the ultrasound wand. Some suck their thumb, and sucking is deemed to be self-soothing as well as preparation for the suck-swallow-breathe rhythm necessary for breastfeeding.

A pregnant mom can calm baby with light stroking of her belly. Others can touch as well, to feel baby's movement. Often, the excited mom will feel a kick and say, "Feel this!" Then it stops. One could frame that as the hand of calm, useful during fussy times after birth. It's worth a try!

While the pregnant mom moved (changed position, perhaps worked night shift) the baby, comfortable in her waterbed of amniotic fluid, was literally a miracle in motion. How strange it must be to a newborn to be put in a still container with no one else's internal sounds or body heat and a whole lot of different degrees of firmness.

Anytime pain or illness or upset exists, being in the arms of Grandma or Mom or Dad is welcome comfort. Symbolic holding, such as enveloping someone with your arms, if not carrying them, applies to older children and adults as well. Connection is a basic human need. Research suggests lots of cuddling can lead to calmness, as well as less anxiety and depression later in life.

What feels good now contributes to later resilience by developing trust in people in the world at large. As you touch or hold a baby, you have new life literally at your fingertips. It is a blessing and a privilege. Bring your past and future thoughts to the present and enjoy the moment. That is a welcome gift at any age.

In addition to the many forms of touch you will naturally initiate, you might try:

- Gentle, long stroking with skin-to-skin contact.
- Rock or bounce baby. He will let you know his preferences.
- Allow baby some independent time. You or he may be too warm for body contact. Restrictive diaper or clothing or unfamiliar style of holding may bother baby, who may benefit from being down on a blanket, perhaps with your hand on his chest or back to indicate your presence.
- Gentle jiggling may settle baby.
- Cross your leg while sitting and bounce baby on your ankle while holding his hands.
- Pay attention to baby's cues to learn what type of touch is welcome in general. A baby who is touched lovingly makes a positive association. He feels lovable and accepted. Rough or jerking motion can elicit fear of falling and therefore aversion to touch. An infant's two initial fears are of falling and loud noise so hold him close to you and educate others who may hold baby

out gingerly believing babies don't like them. Holding baby snugly generally is welcome unless one of you is overheated.

- If you do not have strength to lift or carry baby for long, be creative. Lay him on the couch beside you and play. A baby around four months can sit on the dresser in front of you, cradled by your arms so he can enjoy looking at himself in the mirror. It seems babies like babies as much as grandmothers do. Conserving energy and using your body wisely yields more Grammie Camp adventures.

- Provide a variety of textures for baby to touch such as different fabrics of your clothes, the furniture, or the family dog's fur. Guide baby's hand to feel them.

- Allow for some barefoot time so baby can discover his toes. Diaper-changing time is great for that. When older, let his bare feet feel hardwood, carpet, grass, sand, dry and wet earth, and water that's in addition to bath.

- Bath time gives freedom of movement, awareness of temperature, splashing sensation, and slipperiness of the tub or skin. Talk about all these things and call baby's attention to them.

- Allow baby to squish food through his fingers to explore with his hands and mouth. Ripe banana, avocado, or strawberry appeal. Don't spoil the fun by fussing over tidiness. Protect the floor from inevitable food droppings. A towel or disposable plastic tablecloth under highchair protect carpet. For food on face, a quick swipe with facecloth is enough, no scrubbing. Give him another wet cloth to suck on or soothe gums while you clean his face and hands.

- Provide safe tactile stimulation, such as with a tray of herbs like parsley, a feather, flower, leaf, or a pan of uncooked rice or lentils. In this case, prevent mouthing.

- Gently drape a silk scarf over baby's limbs or face. Put ice cubes and water in a Ziploc bag and baby can feel, watch, and hear new sensations.

Supervise for safety, as with all activities. Babies do not anticipate danger. That is your job.

Greatness comes from great service. Think of your time shared with grandbaby as one of your greatest gifts, to yourself and of yourself. As you practice habitual acts of kindness while you play with baby, you may never know which actions spark brand-new neural connections. All you need to know is that you are a valued contributor in this moment and to this little person's future self. Allow the touching, cuddling, and the tactile experience of caring for baby to develop positive memories and interactions.

A Letter from Grandbaby

Dear Mooey,

I am two weeks old and getting good (so I overhear) at breastfeeding. I am glad you are so smart about that because Mommy seemed to need a lot of help getting us in position since I am so tiny. I didn't mean to cry and upset her and bop my head around. I am just hungry, and it's not always easy. You really help all of us feel calm and know it will all be fine, and we will soon be a great team. It's so satisfying to eat at Mom's. It's not just about food. I can feel the love as I snuggle close to her soft body, and I hear her familiar heartbeat.

Kisses to you!

Olly

Rub-a dub dub, fun in the tub.

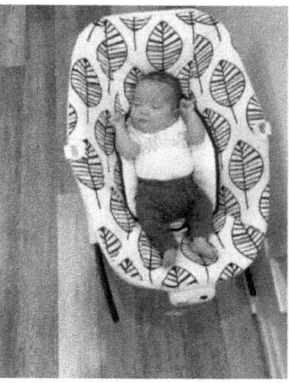
Eat, sleep, grow, and be loved.

We humans are dependent on touch.

Baby is exploring touch and vision.

Nana with this cutie. Boys and their sticks!

Fingers are the best finger food.

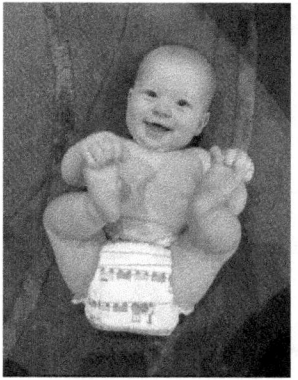
Did you say these toes are mine?

Adventures in Touch

Chapter 10
Adventures in Taste

My tastes are simple: I am easily satisfied with the best.

Winston Churchill

What can a baby taste? Yes, everything that enters the mouth, and not everything is food. Fingers, soothers, blankets, and toys are all taste worthy. Taste buds reside in the tongue, tonsils, and back of the mouth. They identify sweet, sour, bitter, and salty. In 1990, though identified in 1907, umami was validated by the University of Miami as one of the five basic tastes. Baby is exposed to them all in utero while swallowing amniotic fluid, and baby can distinguish between sweet and bitter as early as the first three months. By about twenty weeks gestation, a baby can develop a preference for sweet if the mother has had a high intake of refined sugar. Umami is also present in breast milk, as is the sweetness of lactose. Help your grandbaby discover them all.

Withholding taste sensations that you may not personally care for deprives her of a taste she may enjoy. Often, she doesn't know what she doesn't like until someone—based on their own food preference biases—changes the baby's opinion. That may be through facial expression or distasteful sounds or just not giving a variety of food options. It's amazing how many adults broadly say they don't like vegetables. There are so many to choose from.

Mouthing and tasting new items is not just a reflection of baby's hunger. It's a way that babies learn. Whether edible or not, mouthing is one of his first ways to explore. Babyproof your home and anywhere you are with baby. That may mean hazards remain, but you are on alert. Educate yourself, and do not leave baby unattended. Accidents can happen *very* quickly.

According to Eric Edmeades of Wildfit, a three-month-long health program, there are six human hungers. Often when adults eat, it is for a need other than nutrition, like an empty stomach, low blood sugar, emotional upheaval, variety (boredom), or thirst. All are hungers that may be misread or ignored by desire over need. When you hold some responsibility for nurturing baby, bear these in mind for yourself as a role model as well. Perhaps you associate chocolate chip cookies and milk with your grandmother experience. We impart our values, even in our snack choices.

All behaviour has meaning, yet we often jump to erroneous conclusions. My friend was a nurse in Toronto and could not understand why some Afghan women in the city gave Coca-Cola to their babies. She asked an Afghan nurse, who explained that in a refugee camp, the lack of potable water meant Coca-Cola's high percentage of water, combined with calories from sugar, kept baby alive. It makes sense in that scenario. Mothers made a preferred choice between two poor choices when dehydration was a risk. Though there is no shortage of water in the new country, unlearning habits is difficult.

Food experience, exploration, and exposure—not quantity—is important for baby. Food before a year old is as much for the fun as the nutrition. Include all senses. Social interaction, language, routine, motor development, and sensory development are all part of the eating experience. Mealtime is rich in important learning opportunities.

Eating is a social pastime. It's a multifaceted opportunity to talk about the food, names, colours, textures, where it comes from, and counting food items. A meal can be a whole workshop or learning lab. Be creative. Just because you don't like a particular food should not negate offering it to baby.

With the perks of being a grandmother come the responsibility to do your best to provide only what will ultimately serve your grandbaby's overall health. Notice your own beliefs about food. Does dinner have to include meat and potatoes? What constitutes a breakfast food? Does it have to be cereal from a box? Does one have to finish everything on the plate? Does junk food truly meet your need for comfort or love? It's good for baby to understand her own cues of selection and choice.

Don't be the grandmother who delights in the misguided vision of being a hero by giving baby sugary treats, such as a commercial ice cream cone. You can be a true hero by making homemade ice cream in the blender with frozen berries and cream. Baby can marvel at the transformation before her eyes, and you know the ingredients.

Whether or not baby is eating enough (or too much) can cause much stress for mothers and grandmothers alike. Most babies will consume what their bodies need naturally and normally when provided with age-appropriate options. But when too much focus is placed on eating exact amounts, problems can be created.

Imagine leaving a medical well-baby check-up feeling like a bad mother. One of my community health nurse clients did just that. The family was new to Canada and lacked relatives and friends in the country. The doctor declared the one-year-old significantly underweight and recommended that the mom call public health for guidance. I received the call, was told the baby cried and resisted as Mom approached the highchair with her. Mom had been feeding pureed food, with much resistance from baby, and was likely force-feeding due to her own frustration over getting baby to eat. This mom did well to interpret her baby's cues that feeding was a battle and, being at a loss for a remedy, was wise to seek help.

I visited the next day, having confirmed she had a ripe banana as an option. Sure enough, as she carried the baby toward the highchair, the baby fussed and thrashed. I guided Mom to put a small piece of banana on the highchair tray and back off. The baby devoured it, then another, and another, until the banana was gone, and the baby gave cues for more. A piece of bread was offered next, and baby, with her own hand, ate that. Then she drank milk by cup instead of a bottle.

The mom was amazed and thrilled. She had not known what or how to present food to make the experience enjoyable, or that she should sit with baby at the table and eat something herself (the same food items is ideal). Written resources were left with the very grateful mom, and I expect the baby was grateful as well. The mother could see her baby was hungry, but clearly the baby did not want to be forced to eat pureed food. Baby was ready for more choices and to be allowed to eat independently in her own time frame. In a twenty minute in-person, informative, non-judgmental visit, we may have thwarted an ongoing feeding battle that may have resulted in a poor mother/baby relationship around food and possibly baby's later eating disorder. Instead, Mother's confidence in her mothering skill was boosted, and baby gained independence and pleasure in eating. This is one reason we need to share wisdom and resources. Yay for the doctor's referral, and double yay for the mother reaching out.

Though not an infant, a four-year-old frustrated his mom who sought help because he resisted her getting him dressed. Since she had been raised by servants, she had no idea he needed some independence to learn to dress himself. This is when having exposure to other mothers and children, formally or informally at parks or elsewhere, can save the day.

It doesn't take much to educate a motivated mother. Common sense is not common until it's part of your life experience. Some education about growth and development improved the child's dressing experience for both.

As a grandmother, you will have times when you don't know for sure what the right thing is to do. Use your resources. No one knows everything all the time, and wise is the person who recognizes it and reaches out.

Not everything edible is safe to be eaten. Toxic chemicals are in most homes. Once the baby crawls, you (and baby's parents) should at least once get down on the floor and see what might be there to entice a baby, like that bright container with aromatic dish soap under the sink or that piece of Lego under the couch or the *Dieffenbachia* plant in the corner. All toxic chemicals should be put far out of reach, just to be safe. Learn what houseplants are toxic to babies and pets. Keep unsafe small items that will go into baby's mouth out of view and reach. Check clothing and stuffed toys for loose choking hazards. Be observant.

As new solid foods are introduced, make sure you have cut and prepared them appropriately for baby. Large, round chunks of firm food, like hot dogs and whole grapes, are the perfect throat size and therefore significant choking hazards. Cutting vegetables with a crinkle-cut blade makes them easy to grasp. Later, beyond seven months, the pincer grasp is being developed, so small items, such as blueberries or peas, provide excellent practice for small motor development. A piece of fruit, meat, or vegetable the size of your index finger allows baby a handle and still enough to put into his mouth. Do not give honey under a year because of the potential for botulism spores that adults can handle but babies cannot.

Safety is number one. When baby is first starting solid foods, learn prevention signs and remedies of choking versus gagging. The adult gag reflex is at the back of the mouth, but baby's is halfway back. It is a good protective mechanism in that when baby gags, he tries to get the food back to the front of the tongue, where it can be chewed better or spit out. As you calmly (at least externally) observe gagging, be reassured that sound means baby is okay. Just continue observing. Trying to retrieve it may cause the food to be pushed farther back into the throat.

No sound probably also means no air entry, which means genuine choking is taking place. In this case, time is of the essence. Learn infant CPR and how to manage choking in advance so you will be prepared.

Have emergency numbers and the home address posted by the phone. Sometimes, in crisis, we even forget our own phone numbers.

Mealtime should be a peaceful, social event. Avoid rushed meals as much as possible so baby has time to experience all the tastes that come with the amazing variety of food available to him.

- Offer veggies and fruit. There's no need to offer veggies before fruit. Offer both. You provide, and baby decides what and how much. When variety is offered, baby is more open to trying new things in general.

- Offer sips of water to wash down the food. An open small cup can be managed with help at about five months and skips the need for a bottle. The muscles for this cup-drinking action contribute to muscles needed for speech. Subsequent use of a sippy cup and straws also engage and strengthen muscles used in speech.

- Plan finger foods that both baby and you can eat to model your enjoyment.

- Relax, smile, become childlike, celebrate mealtime. Don't wait for special occasions or birthdays. Make every day special.

- Be aware that the best predictor of feeding enjoyment is the adult's attitude toward it.

- Compare your grandbaby to your grandbaby, not any chart or expectation. Each milestone has a typical age range for expected achievement, but there will always be babies developing skills before and after. Peer pressure and bragging can add unnecessary stress. Follow baby's cues about what foods to try next.

- Make a list of treats for your baby that are not sugary and that his parents endorse. Help your grandbaby cultivate the taste for nutritious foods by giving only nutritious options.

- Expect a mess in baby's learning to feed himself. Celebrate the joy of the food experience. If you keep wiping baby's mouth or hands throughout the feeding, it takes some of the fun out of it.

Bonding time is anytime—being together, playing together, eating together, or even changing diaper. It does not need to include snack food, but it can. Use mealtime as an opportunity to engage all of baby's senses, but taste will certainly top the list. Provide a healthy variety of choices, and let baby learn what she loves. Time spent with you will be on the top of the list.

A Letter from Grandbaby

Dear Abuela,

You know how I love adventures with you. Today was a whole new type with Mom and Dad. I had my first feel and taste of your favourite green food: avocado. I know we grow the most avocados right here in Mexico. That makes me proud. So, I could hardly wait. I have been watching Mom and Dad put all kinds of things in their mouths. Everything I can put my hands on goes into my mouth. I love the feel and sometimes the taste (and sometimes not!). My moose makes crinkly noises when I chew on him.

So, they decided to try my first solids on the weekend so Mom could do the food and Dad could do the pictures and videos. Today was the big day. I sat in my highchair in just a diaper. I was swinging my legs, excited for what was to happen. Slices of avocado, I found out, are soft in my mouth and squishy in my fingers, and I was excited. Except, it was cold. That was a surprise. Mom's superpower is to feed me her milk at a nice warm temperature—just like she is, warm and familiar. I hope they don't get the avocado from the fridge next time. Thank you for the special knife you gave Mom, so the pieces were grooved and easy to hold. I am so clever, as you know. You tell me that all the time. I am smart. I am clever. I learn so fast. I like when you say those things about me.

So, it was a great adventure. We all had fun. I can hardly wait until you visit next week, and we can both eat avocado.

Love,

Your Special Sobrina,

Juanita

So much learning to digest!

Baby as she ventures into solid foods.

Mother Nature and mother give baby the best nourishment.

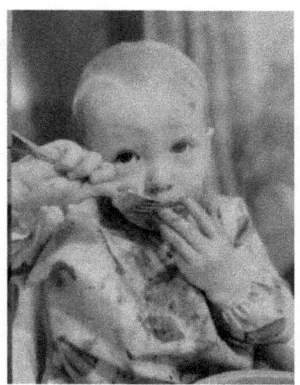
Grammie Camp says finger foods are fun.

Baby, wearing her favorite food, the avocado.

Adventures in Taste

Chapter 11
Adventures in Smell

Of the five senses, smell is the one with the best memory.

Rebecca McClanahan, author

Our olfactory or smelling system is so powerful, and is in the middle of the brain, very close to our memory centre. No wonder smells elicit strong memories. If you and baby walk often near a cow pasture or by the cookie factory or a restaurant featuring fried chicken and you chat and enjoy each other, future whiffs of manure, sugar, and cooking oil may flood that older baby's brain with an unexpected sense of happiness forever after.

You, Grandma, may smell of perfume or soap or garlic or your own body oil. Whatever it is, your grandbaby can smell your unique aroma: *eau de grandma*. Do you have strong memories associated with specific people? Cigar smoke of a favourite uncle, the perfume of an aunt, the bread factory in town? Be aware of what scent will remind your grandbaby of you.

A baby's olfactory cells begin to develop in the first trimester of pregnancy and likely baby can smell in the last trimester (as presumed by studies of preterm babies and animals). He can learn his mother's smell through inhaling the amniotic fluid, which contains essence of what his mother ate or even chemicals from beauty products that go into the bloodstream and then the amniotic fluid. This baby may like garlic more if his mom ate a lot of garlic than does a baby who did not already sample spices in utero. Often, new parents ask if it's okay to add spices to baby's food. Assume baby has already been exposed to Mom's food choices and don't worry.

A newborn can, with eyes closed, wriggle tummy to tummy on Mom, find his way to the breast, and, with patient non-interference, latch onto the nipple. He just follows his crawling instincts and the scent of Mom's milk. Initial action may be more licking than sucking, but taste and smell are very closely linked. A baby can, within days of birth, distinguish between his own mother's milk and another's, but the specific fragrances of breastmilk are very appealing to babies in general.

A newborn baby's scent memory lasts a few weeks—a good reason to be with your grandbaby early. Recent research suggests a newborn's odour activates reward and pleasure centres in the brain, so Mom seeks more of her baby and the baby seeks more of Mom. I learned that my newborn's sweet breastfed-baby smell elicited joy in a midwife, who greeted me with outstretched arms saying, "I just love the smell of breastfed babies!"

My very verbal two-year-old was not in agreement with my plan of stopping breastfeeding, despite two weeks' notice. It was not us as the nursing pair, but the peer pressure that created the deadline in that time and circle of family and friends. The toddler pleaded, "I just want to hold them. I just want to smell them." Clearly, there's more to breastfeeding than nutrition.

How can you create olfactory adventures in Grammie Camp?

- Be cognizant of your scents of cologne, detergent, and deodorant that may irritate baby's skin or nose, as evidenced by sniffles, red eyes, or rashes.

- After six months, offer a tray of safe herbs for baby to smell and manipulate and potentially taste, like mint or parsley.

- In the garden or woods, hold a flower close to baby's nose and say, "This lilac flower smells so sweet." Match smell descriptions with language.

- When passing a freshly cut lawn, comment that it smells like someone cut the grass.

- When cooking, say, "It smells like chicken. Mmm. Do you want chicken for lunch?"

- When you notice a smell, name it.

- When baby's diaper is smelly, refrain from saying, "Pee-u. You smell stinky," with a look and sound of disgust. Would you want someone judging you?

- On a cold, wintry day, you might comment, "My nose is cold. I smell the car warming up in the driveway. It's a strong smell."

Every experience is a learning opportunity. So many neural connections are being made in baby's first year. Create many opportunities to multiply and enrich those connections. Remember that play is a child's work. It is key to learning not just facts but confidence and well-being and how he fits in with the world. Purposeful and intentional activities need not be structured. Some of life's most poignant memories are impromptu or impulsive. Carpe diem! If a storm cancels your picnic plan, pray for thunder and pretend you are an animal roaring or grumbling. By providing options and reading baby's interest cues, you can gauge how much of what activities are most appropriate and enjoyed, and the joy of learning, doing, and just *being* all contribute to retention and positive memories.

A Letter from Grandbaby

Nonna,

Do you believe I am seven months old already? Mom says I am growing up too fast because now I can crawl, and my crib got moved into my own room. How can I grow too fast? You say God has a plan. So far, I like the plan.

I love our outdoor adventures. Tonight, when you carried me in the front pack (which I love because I can see where we are going), it was dark and quiet and no one else was out walking. Then you pointed out something walking in the middle of the road coming toward us. You whispered it might be a cat or a skunk or a raccoon. It was slow and waddling. So, we stood still, and it kept coming. I don't think it saw us watching. Then it turned into the driveway, looked at us, then scooted behind a car into the woods. You said it was a raccoon and it probably smelled us. I didn't know we smelled. I wonder what I smell like. I didn't smell the raccoon. You said that was likely who ripped open the bag of kitchen scraps Mom left outside the door last night and forgot to take to the compost bin. Nonna, how do you know everything? Did he smell that too? I want to be smart like you. Maybe I need to grow up faster.

Ti amo,

Travis

It smells as good as it looks.

Grammie Camp philosophy says explore everything together.

Curiosity feeds more than the imagination.

Adventures in Smell

Chapter 12
The End of One and Beginning of Two

You only grow by coming to the end of something and by beginning something else.

John Irving, The World According to Garp

Can you believe how much more you know now about infancy than you did a year ago? As you continue to strengthen the bond between yourself and your grandbaby, you continually are reminded that it's the caring, the doing (even diaper changing), and the being—while smiling, talking, cuddling, engaging—which strengthen the bond. Be proud of how you have invested in this impressionable little person. Imagine your grandbaby is now one year old. How did time go so fast as you have been living your dream of being a grandmother cherished by this baby? You both are blessed, and you can take pride in knowing you are instrumental in a special part of her growing.

The end of infancy launches toddlerhood, in which you can have just as significant a role, having laid the foundation of your strong, loving connection.

A one-year-old's development promises a new learning curve with twists and turns with a whole different depth and breadth of ways of spending joyous times together. As you create the evolving Grammie Camp experiences you both love, you might ponder Jiminy Cricket soulfully and sweetly reminding us that any wish can come true.

May the miraculous grandmother that you are always bring the power of love to the person your grandson or granddaughter is becoming. The possibilities are limitless! Each of you is blessed and a blessing within your relationship. You are valued as well as valuable in your investment in Grammie Camp. I recall so much love and time dedicated to my first child, wondering how it could possibly be sufficiently multiplied for additional children. Mother Nature is very clever. I learned each child has a different experience of being parented because each is unique in the moment. Your time and energy may change, yet the happiness of giving of yourself and receiving unknown rewards for each of you is somehow magnified. Your smile and love and intentional gifting of shared time will never be diminished. You are needed. Enjoy the ever-changing ride!

First Year Resources

Resources for parenting are as numerous as there are parents—often conflicting and always biased. We *all* are biased by our life experience, culture, education—even if we think not. My suggestion as a community health nurse, mother, and grandmother has always been to listen, to read, to observe, then try whatever makes sense to you. No need to defend your methods. You will soon know what works, what doesn't, and have the option of choosipline at your service. As in fashions in clothing, there are fashions in parenting styles. Message sent with good intentions does not equate with message received as welcome. Typically, people share how they did things and therefore assume it's correct and universal. That includes your doctor and other professionals. We humans are very human in that regard!

Grandmothers apparently are so resourceful as to have little written about them! Hence my offerings in this book and encouragement to share your wisdom far and wide.

Below are just a few of the specific resources valued by myself and my daughter during my grandson's first year. Watching a feeding video together reassured my daughter I was up to date.

Many resources are free. Sources of resources are:

Previous experience with infants, recollection of how you were parented, or experienced grandmothers.

Peers, parents. Some research shows mothers trust other mothers over other resources with the assumption, perhaps, that mothers are more up to date on topics such as infant feeding and sleep guidelines.

Library, community centres, early childhood centres, and public health departments for online or in-person prenatal and parenting classes.

Instagram has some free bite-size content that is handy while nursing or rocking baby or other activities as well as links to videos and programs with cost. Among the Instagram resources are:

- Feeding Littles
- Solid Starts
- Taking Cara Babies
- Raising Little Talkers (language development)
- Kids Eat in Color (infant feeding plus strategies for older picky eaters)
- Curious Neuron Podcast

- Gentle Parenting (breaking generational trauma in parenting choices and behaviour)
- Huckleberry (Instagram photos, videos, and applications on cell phones for tracking sleep, feeds, diapers, growth, meds. There is both a free version plus upgrade with cost.)
- The Wonder Weeks (development milestones)

Google has so much (too much?) information with so many ways to spiral into overload and use excess time that is already at a premium.

Jumping from Grandma's arms and into the future!

Looking back on infancy, now a toddler.

Immersion in our family's third generation of camp.

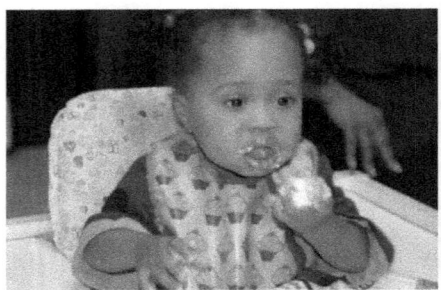
End of year one, from infant to toddler.

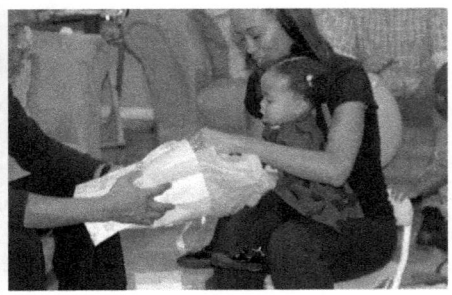
First birthday! Looking to the future.

Grammie Camp celebrates,
connects, and raises happiness.

References

Barnard Center for Infant Health and Development: *Your Baby & You. Attachment in the First Year. Video for Parents and Guide for Professionals.* Seattle, Washington. 2011. Many printed and online resources to learn about infant caregiving.

Barnard. University of Washington School of Nursing and Center on Human Development & Disability. DVD. Baby Cues® A Child's First Language. Seattle. 2nd Edition. 2019. Pcrprograms.org/pcrp@uw.edu

Brazelton, T. Barry, MD with Joshua D. Sparrow, MD *Touchpoints Birth to Three. Your Child's Emotional and Behavioral Development.* Cambridge, Massachusetts. Da Capo Press. 2006.

Holy Bible, New King James Version. Nashville: Thomas Nelson, Inc., 2013 1 Corinthians 13:13 and 13:12.

Proctor, Bob. You Were Born Rich. Revised Edition 2015. Proctor Gallagher Institute. Phoenix, Arizona. www.proctorgallagherinstitute.com. Masterclass coaching group 2021.

Rhodes, Monique; http://www.moniquerhodes.com; varied courses to increase happiness by using mind. The Power House coaching group 2021-2022. "Power House Mastermind" 2022-2023

Shimoff, Marci with Kline, Carol. *Happy for No Reason: 7 steps to Being Happy from the Inside Out.* New York. Atria Books. 2013. Book, Heather Hobbs-Certified Happy for No Reason Trainer™. Feb 2023

Author Accolades

One need not be a baby to learn that every milestone is preceded by many steps.

Accolades go out to all the worldwide photographers who captured moments in time which we chose to enrich this book.

Pictures as well as words speak volumes.

Represented in photographs are:

Adam Cully, Akshay Gandhi, Amy, BL, Brian Wildcat, Claire Louise Hobbs, Cathy Gross, D. Parkhill, Devon, Dianne Cully, D.Hobbs, Dorothy Zajac, Edith Hobbs, EL, Gail Russell, Gladys, GGMa Maur, Gramma, Grandma Winn, Grandy, Granny, Gwyn, Heather Dahmer, Heather Henry, Heather Hobbs, IP, Jack Livingston, Jacob Cully, Jakob, James, Jennifer, JL, Josie, Julia Farquharson, June, June., Kelleigh, L., Laurel Hobbs, Lenore, Lilah Jones, Lily, Linda Wheler, Lindsey Leamen, Mak, Marion Miller, Martha Leamen, Max, M. Allison, Melanie Henry, Moira, Nana, Nanny, and Lucianne Dobson with Luka Deryk Senicar-Dobson, Jacquie Ray, and Stella Birkett.

Nana Gwen Curtis with granddaughter Alison and son Logan, Nana Patti Clark with granddaughters June and Carrie.

Also photographed are Olly, Oma, Paighton, P.P., P.E.M., Parker Hamlett, Quinn Hamlett, Randy Leamen, Roberta Canning, S. Dennis, Tadhg, Thomas, Travis Leamen, Trent, Tundra, Vaani, Vinaya, WL, and Wynken.

Whew! That's a lot of love!

I would also like to thank Grandmothers to Grandmothers Campaign for their ongoing labours of love with funds going to African grandmothers and who will receive a portion of profits from book sales.

I am grateful to GracePoint Publishing for their premise that it's *my* book, so their strategic questions and gentle suggestions guided its transformation. Because I am a visual learner and teacher, photo credits are first; however, the crucial steps in the manuscript were guided by developmental editor Meg Welch Dendler and further fine-tuned by GracePoint team of senior editor Laurie Knight, director of publishing Tascha Yoder, and interior designer Ariel Austill from draft to finale.

Hallelujah! It was a long labour, and the book was born. May it adventure around the world sharing wisdom and joy all the while.

Heather Hobbs

Heather Hobbs is a retired community health nurse with a Bachelor of Science in Nursing from the University of Toronto and certificates in Solution Focused Counselling and Solution Focused Coaching. She is also trained as a facilitator for grief support groups.

The majority of her career was spent as a community health nurse and childbirth educator in Canada at rural and urban homes, libraries, schools, and Early Years Centers in Alberta and Ontario. Although pre and postpartum groups and Transition to Parenting groups took place in community settings, the bulk of her work in supporting new and young families was during home visits. Together, Heather and her soulmate Randy, raised three stellar children, Lindsey, Katie, and Travis. Heather is now the happy Grammie to grandson, Jacob, and three granddogs.

Actively engaged in her community through volunteer work as a summer camp nurse and varied volunteer duties at local theatres, Heather nurtures friendships far and wide. As a newly certified Happy for No Reason Trainer™, Heather sees grandmothers as a priority for workshops to elevate and strengthen happiness.

This book is for all the grandmothers who artfully and playfully help their grandbabies grow while serving their mutual need for connection, love, and a sense of being valued.

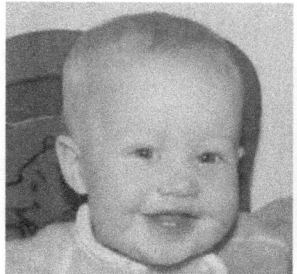

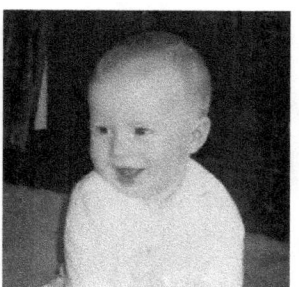

They grow up so fast!

You can choose to be an active participant or passive bystander. Seize the moment and create adventures that Grammiehood can provide.

Comment with Heather at: www.grammiecamp.ca

Email: heatherhobbs.author@gmail.com

Your wisdom is welcome!

For more great books from Peak Press
Visit Books.GracePointPublishing.com

If you enjoyed reading *Grammie Camp,* and purchased it through an online retailer, please return to the site and write a review to help others find the book.

www.ingramcontent.com/pod-product-compliance
Lightning Source LLC
Chambersburg PA
CBHW050554160426
43199CB00015B/2662